Science Fare— Chemistry at the Table

Science in Our World
Volume One

☑ **W9-DJD-678**

Developed in collaboration with

Procter & Gamble

Series Editor
Mickey Sarquis, Director
Center for Chemical Education

Instructional Resource Material
University of Delaware
Mathematics & Science Education Resource Center
105 Pearson Hall
Newark, DE 19716

©1995 by Terrific Science Press
ISBN 1-883822-12-2 First printed 1995 Revised and reprinted 1997
All rights reserved. Printed in the United States of America.

This project was supported, in part, by the National Science Foundation. Any opinions, findings, and conclusions or recommendations expressed in this material are those of the authors and do not necessarily reflect the views of the National Science Foundation. The Government has certain rights to this material. This material is based upon work supported by the National Science Foundation under Grant No. TPE-9153930.

Center for
Chemical Education

This monograph is intended for use by teachers, chemists, and properly supervised students. Teachers and other users must develop and follow procedures for the safe handling, use, and disposal of chemicals in accordance with local and state regulations and requirements. The cautions, warnings, and safety reminders associated with the doing of experiments and activities involving the use of chemicals and equipment contained in this publication have been compiled from sources believed to be reliable and to represent the best opinion on the subject as of 1995. However, no warranty, guarantee, or representation is made by the editor, contributors, Procter & Gamble, or the Terrific Science Press as to the correctness or sufficiency of any information herein. Neither the editor, contributors, Procter & Gamble, or the Terrific Science Press assumes any responsibility or liability for the use of the information herein, nor can it be assumed that all necessary warnings and precautionary measures are contained in this publication. Other or additional information or measures may be required or desirable because of particular or exceptional conditions or circumstances, or because of new or changed legislation.

Contributors

Industrial Mentors

Dave Henry
Research Chemist, Food & Beverage Sector
Winton Hill Technical Center, Procter & Gamble
Cincinnati, Ohio

Dick DePalma
Research Chemist, Food & Beverage Sector
Winton Hill Technical Center, Procter & Gamble
Cincinnati, Ohio

Academic Mentors

Sally Vonderbrink
Chemistry Teacher, St. Xavier High School
Cincinnati, Ohio

Jeanne Buccigross*
Chemistry Professor, Department of Chemistry
College of Mount St. Joseph
Cincinnati, Ohio

Pat Koochaki*
Chemistry Professor, Department of Chemistry
Raymond Walters College, Cincinnati, Ohio
Procter & Gamble, Cincinnati, Ohio

Peer Mentor

Debbie Mears*
General Science Teacher, Franklin Junior High School
Franklin, Ohio

* Photo not available.

Principal Investigators

Mickey Sarquis	Miami University, Middletown, Ohio
Jim Coats	Dow Chemical USA (retired), Findlay, Ohio
Dan McLoughlin	Xavier University, Cincinnati, Ohio
Rex Bucheit	Fillmore Elementary School, Hamilton, Ohio

Partners for Terrific Science Advisory Board

Ruby L. Bryant	Colonel White High School, Dayton, Ohio
Rex Bucheit	Fillmore Elementary School (ex-officio), Hamilton, Ohio
Jim Coats	Dow Chemical USA (retired, ex-officio), Findlay, Ohio
Dick French	Quantum Chemical Corporation (retired, ex-officio), Cincinnati, Ohio
Judy Gilbert	BP America/Ohio Chemical Council, Lima, Ohio
Linda Jester	John XXIII Elementary School, Middletown, Ohio
James C. Letton	Procter & Gamble, Cincinnati, Ohio
Ted J. Logan	Procter & Gamble, Ross, Ohio
Ken Lohr	Hoechst Marion Roussel, Inc. (retired), Cincinnati, Ohio
Alan McClelland	Delaware Science Alliance (DuPont, retired), Rockland, Delaware (deceased)
Dan McLoughlin	Xavier University (ex-officio), Cincinnati, Ohio
Raymond C. Odioso	R.C. Odioso Consultants, Inc. (Drackett, retired), Cincinnati, Ohio, St. Petersburg Beach, Florida
Tom Runyan	Garfield Alternative School, Middletown, Ohio
Ken Wilkinson	Hilton Davis Company (retired), Cincinnati, Ohio
John P. Williams	Miami University Hamilton, Hamilton, Ohio
Regina Wolterman	Our Lady of Lourdes Elementary School, Cincinnati, Ohio

Table of Contents

Acknowledgments

The authors and editor wish to thank the following individuals who have contributed to the development of the *Science in Our World* series of Teacher Resource Modules.

Terrific Science Press Design and Production Team
Susan Gertz, Amy Stander, Lisa Taylor, Thomas Nackid, Stephen Gentle, Vickie Fultz, Anne Munson, Amy Hudepohl, Andrea Nolan, Pamela Mason

Reviewers
Susan Hershberger	Miami University, Oxford, Ohio
Baird Lloyd	Miami University, Middletown, Ohio
Diane Rose	Ursuline Academy, Cincinnati, Ohio
Mark Sabo	Miami University, Middletown, Ohio
Dave Tomlin	Wright Patterson Air Force Base, Dayton, Ohio
Linda Woodward	University of Southwestern Louisiana, Lafayette, Louisiana

Center for Chemical Education Staff

Mickey Sarquis, Director
Bruce L. Peters, Jr., Associate Director
Billie Gerzema, Administrative Assistant

Assistants to Director
Susan Gertz	Mark Sabo
Lynn Hogue	Lisa Meeder Turnbull

Project Coordinators and Managers
Richard French	Andrea Nolan
Betty Kibbey	Ginger Smith
Carl Morgan	Amy Stander

Research Associates and Assistants
Kersti Cox	Pamela Mason
Stephen Gentle	Anne Munson
Susan Hershberger	Thomas Nackid
Amy Hudepohl	Michael Parks
Robert Hunter	Lisa Taylor

Program Secretaries
Victoria Burton	Ruth Willis

Graduate Assistants
Michelle Diebolt	Richard Rischling
Nancy Grim	Michella Stultz

Foreword

Science Fare—Chemistry at the Table is one of the *Science in Our World* Teacher Resource Modules. This set is aimed at enabling teachers to introduce their students to the concepts and processes of industrial chemistry and to relate these concepts to the consumer products students encounter daily. These hands-on, problem-solving activities help connect science lessons with real life.

Developed as a collaborative effort between industrial, academic, and teacher peer mentors in the *Partners for Terrific Science* program, this module provides background information on the food industry and Procter & Gamble's role in this industry, as well as a content review of food science and pedagogical strategies. The activities in this module have been tested by participants in *Partners* programs and by *Partners* teachers in their classrooms, and reviewed by experts in the field to help ensure accuracy, safety, and pedagogical effectiveness.

Partners for Terrific Science, established in 1986, is an industrial/academic partnership that facilitates interaction among classroom teachers, industrial scientists and engineers, and university chemistry faculty to make science education more interesting, relevant, and understandable for all students. The partnership is supported by the Ohio Chemical Council and its more than 100 members, the National Science Foundation, the U.S. Department of Education, the Ohio Board of Regents, the American Chemical Society—Cincinnati Section, Miami University, and over 50 private-sector partners. Procter & Gamble has generously contributed to the production of this module.

This *Science in Our World* series represents the collaborative efforts of these industrial chemists and educators. The Teacher Resource Modules have been developed especially for teachers who want to use industry-based physical science activities in the classroom, but who may not have been able to attend a *Partners* workshop at the Miami site or one of the Affiliate sites nationwide. We want to thank all the contributors, participants, and mentors who made this publication possible.

We hope you will find that these Teacher Resource Modules provide you with a useful and exciting way to involve your students in doing chemistry through integrated real-world themes. We welcome your comments at any time and are interested in learning about especially successful uses of these materials.

Mickey Sarquis, Director
Center for Chemical Education
July 1995

The Center for Chemical Education

Built on a tradition of quality programming, materials development, and networking between academia and industry, Miami University's Center for Chemical Education (CCE) encompasses a multifaceted collaboration of cross-grade-level and interdisciplinary initiatives begun in the mid-1980s as Terrific Science Programs. These initiatives are linked through the centrality of chemistry to the goal of fostering quality hands-on, minds-on science education for all students. CCE activities include credit coursework and other opportunities for educators at all levels; K–12 student programs; undergraduate, graduate, and postgraduate programs in chemical education; materials development, including teacher resource materials, program handbooks, and videos; public outreach efforts and networking to foster new and existing partnerships among classroom teachers, university-based science educators, industrial scientists, and professional societies.

Professional Development for Educators

Credit Courses   The Center for Chemical Education offers a variety of summer and academic-year workshop-style courses for K–12 and college teachers. While each workshop has a unique focus, all reflect current pedagogical approaches in science education, cutting-edge academic and industrial research topics, and classroom applications for teachers and students. Short courses provide opportunities for educators to enrich their science teaching in a limited amount of time. All courses offer graduate credit.

Non-Credit Courses   Academies allow CCE graduates and other teachers to attend special one-day sessions presented by leading science educators from around the United States. Offerings include seminars, mini-workshops, and share-and-swap sessions.

Internships   Through 8- to 10-week summer internships, program graduates work as members of industrial teams to gain insight into the day-to-day workings of industrial laboratories, enabling them to bring real-world perspectives into the classroom.

Fellowships   Master teachers at primary, secondary, and college levels do research in chemical education and undertake curriculum and materials development as Teacher Fellows with the Center for Chemical Education. Fellowships are available for the summer and the academic year.

K–12 Student Programming

Summer Camps   A variety of summer camps are available to area elementary, middle, and high school students. These camps not only provide laboratory-based enrichment for students, but also enable educators in summer courses to apply their knowledge of hands-on exploration and leadership skills. Satellite camps are offered at affiliated sites throughout the country.

Science Carnivals   Carnivals challenge elementary school students with hands-on science in a non-traditional atmosphere, encouraging them to apply the scientific method to activities that demonstrate scientific principles. Sponsoring teachers and their students host these carnivals for other students in their districts.

Super Saturday Science Sessions	High school students are introduced to industrial and research applications of science and technology through special Saturday sessions that involve the students in experiment-based problem-solving. Topics have included waste management, environmental sampling, engineering technology, paper science, chemical analysis, microbiology, and many others.
Ambassador Program	Professional chemists, technicians, and engineers, practicing and recently retired, play important roles as classroom ambassadors for high school and two-year college students. Ambassadors not only serve as classroom resources, but they are also available as consultants when a laboratory scenario calls for outside expertise; they mentor special projects both in and out of the classroom; and they are available for career counseling and professional advice.

Undergraduate and Graduate Student Programming

Teaching Science with TOYS Undergraduate Course	This undergraduate course replicates the Teaching Science with TOYS teacher inservice program for the preservice audience. Students participate in hands-on physics and chemistry sessions.
General Chemistry Initiative	This effort is aimed at more effectively including chemical analysis and problem solving in the two-year college curriculum. To accomplish this goal, we are developing and testing discovery-based laboratory scenarios and take-home lecture supplements that illustrate topics in chemistry through activities beyond the classroom. In addition to demonstrating general chemistry concepts, these activities also involve students in critical-thinking and group problem-solving skills used by professional chemists in industry and academia.
Chemical Technology Curriculum Development	Curriculum and materials development efforts highlight the collaboration between college and high school faculty and industrial partners. These efforts will lead to the dissemination of a series of activity-based monographs, including detailed instructions for discovery-based investigations that challenge students to apply principles of chemical technology, chemical analysis, and Good Laboratory Practices in solving problems that confront practicing chemical technicians in the workplace.
Other Undergraduate Activities	The CCE has offered short courses/seminars for undergraduates that are similar in focus and pedagogy to CCE teacher/faculty enhancement programming. In addition, CCE staff members provide Miami University students with opportunities to interact in area schools through public outreach efforts and to undertake independent study projects in chemical education.
Degree Program	Miami's Department of Chemistry offers both a Ph.D. and M.S. in Chemical Education for graduate students who are interested in becoming teachers of chemistry in situations where a comprehensive knowledge of advanced chemical concepts is required and where acceptable scholarly activity can include the pursuit of chemical education research.

Educational Materials

The Terrific Science Press publications have emerged from CCE's work with classroom teachers of grades K–12 and college in graduate-credit, workshop-style inservice courses. Before being released, our materials undergo extensive classroom testing by teachers working with students at the targeted grade level, peer review by experts in the field for accuracy and safety, and editing by a staff of technical writers for clear, accurate, and consistent materials lists and procedures. The following is a list of Terrific Science Press publications to date.

Science Activities for Elementary Classrooms (1986)

Science SHARE is a resource for busy K–6 teachers to enable them to use hands-on science activities in their classrooms. The activities included use common, everyday materials and complement or supplement any existing science curriculum. This book was published in collaboration with Flinn Scientific, Inc.

Polymers All Around You! (1992)

This monograph focuses on the uses of polymer chemistry in the classroom. It includes several multi-part activities dealing with topics such as polymer recycling and polymers and polarized light. This monograph was published in collaboration with POLYED, a joint education committee of two divisions of the American Chemical Society: the Division of Polymer Chemistry and the Division of the Polymeric Materials: Science and Engineering.

Fun with Chemistry Volume 2 (1993)

The second volume of a set of two hands-on activity collections, this book contains classroom-tested science activities that enhance teaching, are fun to do, and help make science relevant to young students. This book was published in collaboration with the Institute for Chemical Education (ICE), University of Wisconsin-Madison.

Santa's Scientific Christmas (1993)

In this school play for elementary students, Santa's elves teach him the science behind his toys. The book and accompanying video provide step-by-step instructions for presenting the play. The book also contains eight fun, hands-on science activities to do in the classroom.

Teaching Chemistry with TOYS Teaching Physics with TOYS (1995)

Each volume contains more than 40 activities for grades K–9. Both were developed in collaboration with and tested by classroom teachers from around the country. These volumes were published in collaboration with McGraw-Hill, Inc.

Palette of Color Monograph Series (1995)

The three monographs in this series present the chemistry behind dye colors and show how this chemistry is applied in "real-world" settings:
- The Chemistry of Vat Dyes
- The Chemistry of Natural Dyes
- The Chemistry of Food Dyes

Science in Our World Teacher Resource Modules (1995)

Each volume of this five-volume set presents chemistry activities based on a specific industry—everything from pharmaceuticals to polymers. Developed as a result of the *Partners for Terrific Science* program, this set explores the following topics and industries:
- Science Fare—Chemistry at the Table (Procter & Gamble)
- Strong Medicine—Chemistry at the Pharmacy (Hoechst Marion Roussel, Inc.)
- Dirt Alert—The Chemistry of Cleaning (Diversey Corporation)
- Fat Chance—The Chemistry of Lipids (Henkel Corporation, Emery Group)
- Chain Gang—The Chemistry of Polymers (Quantum Chemical Corporation)

Teaching Physical Science through Children's Literature (1996)	This book offers 20 complete lessons for teaching hands-on, discovery-oriented physical science in the elementary classroom using children's fiction and nonfiction books as an integral part of that instruction. Each lesson in this book is a tightly integrated learning episode with a clearly defined science content objective supported and enriched by all facets of the lesson, including reading of both fiction and nonfiction, writing, and, where appropriate, mathematics. Along with the science content objectives, many process objectives are woven into every lesson.
Teaching Science with TOYS Teacher Resource Modules (1996, 1997)	The modules in this series are designed as instructional units focusing on a given theme or content area in chemistry or physics. Built around a collection of grade-level-appropriate TOYS activities, each Teacher Resource Module also includes a content review and pedagogical strategies section. Volumes listed below were published or are forthcoming in collaboration with McGraw-Hill, Inc. • Exploring Matter with TOYS: Using and Understanding the Senses • Investigating Solids, Liquids, and Gases with TOYS: States of Matter and Changes of State • Transforming Energy with TOYS: Mechanical Energy and Energy Conversions

Terrific Science Network

Affiliates	College and district affiliates to CCE programs disseminate ideas and programming throughout the United States. Program affiliates offer support for local teachers, including workshops, resource/symposium sessions, and inservices; science camps; and college courses.
Industrial Partners	We collaborate directly with over 40 industrial partners, all of whom are fully dedicated to enhancing the quality of science education for teachers and students in their communities and beyond. A list of corporations and organizations that support *Partners for Terrific Science* is included on the following page.
Outreach	On the average, graduates of CCE professional development programs report reaching about 40 other teachers through district inservices and other outreach efforts they undertake. Additionally, graduates, especially those in facilitator programs, institute their own local student programs. CCE staff also undertake significant outreach through collaboration with local schools, service organizations, professional societies, and museums.
Newsletters	CCE newsletters provide a vehicle for network communication between program graduates, members of industry, and other individuals active in chemical and science education. Newsletters contain program information, hands-on science activities, teacher resources, and ideas on how to integrate hands-on science into the curriculum.

For more information about any of the CCE initiatives, contact us at

Center for Chemical Education
4200 East University Blvd.
Middletown, OH 45042
513/727-3318
FAX: 513/727-3223
e-mail: *CCE@muohio.edu*
http://www.muohio.edu/~ccecwis/

Partnership Network

We appreciate the dedication and contributions of the following corporations and organizations, who together make *Partners for Terrific Science* a true partnership for the betterment of chemical education for all teachers and students.

Partners in the Private Sector

A & B Foundry, Inc.
Aeronca, Inc.
Ag Renu
Air Products and Chemicals, Inc.
Armco, Inc.
Armco Research and Technology
ARW Polywood
Ashland Chemical Company
Bank One
BASF
Bay West Paper Corporation
Black Clawson Company
BP America: BP Oil, BP Chemicals
Coats & Clark
Crystal Tissue Company
DataChem Laboratories, Inc.
Diversey Corporation
Ronald T. Dodge Company
Dover Chemical Corporation
Dow Chemical USA
Fluor Daniel Fernald, Inc.
Formica
Henkel Corporation, Emery Group

Hewlett-Packard Company
Hilton Davis Company
Hoechst Marion Roussel, Inc.
Inland Container Corporation
Jefferson Smurfit Corporation
JLJ, Inc.
Magnode Corporation
Middletown Paperboard Corporation
Middletown Regional Hospital
Middletown Wastewater Treatment Plant
Middletown Water Treatment Plant
Miller Brewing Company
The Monsanto Fund
Owens Corning Science & Technology Laboratories
The Procter & Gamble Company
Quality Chemicals
Quantum Chemical Corporation
Rumpke Waste Removal/Recycling
Shepherd Chemical Company
Shepherd Color Company
Sorg Paper Company
Square D Company
Sun Chemical Corporation

Partners in the Public Sector

Hamilton County Board of Education
Indiana Tech-Prep
Miami University
Middletown Clean Community
National Institute of Environmental Health Sciences
National Science Foundation
Ohio Board of Regents, Columbus, OH

Ohio Department of Education
Ohio Environmental Protection Agency
Ohio Tech-Prep
State Board for Technical and Comprehensive Education, Columbia, SC
US Department of Education
US Department of Energy, Cincinnati, OH

Professional Societies

American Association of Physics Teachers
African American Math-Science Coalition
American Chemical Society— Central Regional Council
American Chemical Society— Cincinnati Section
American Chemical Society— Dayton Section
American Chemical Society—POLYED
American Chemical Society— Technician Division
American Chemical Society, Washington, DC

American Institute of Chemical Engineers
Chemical Manufacturers Association
Chemistry Teachers Club of New York
Intersocietal Polymer and Plastics Education Initiative
Minorities in Mathematics, Science and Engineering
National Organization of Black Chemists and Chemical Engineers—Cincinnati Section
National Science Teachers Association
Ohio Chemical Council
Science Education Council of Ohio
Society of Plastics Engineers

More than 3,000 teachers are involved in and actively benefiting from this Network.

An Invitation to Industrial Chemists

It is not unusual to hear children say they want to be doctors, astronauts, or teachers when they grow up. It is easy for children to see adults they admire doing these jobs in books, on television, and in real life. But where are our aspiring chemists? The chemist portrayed on television often bears close resemblance to Mr. Hyde: an unrealistic and unfortunate role model.

Children delight in learning and enjoy using words like "stegosaurus" and "pterodactyl." Wouldn't it be wonderful to hear words like "chromatography" and "density" used with the same excitement? You could be introducing elementary school students to these words for the first time. And imagine a 10-year-old child coming home from school and announcing, "When I grow up, I want to be a chemist!" You can be the one responsible for such enthusiasm. By taking the time to visit and interact with an elementary or middle school classroom as a guest scientist, you can become the chemist who makes the difference.

You are probably aware that many non-chemists, including many prehigh school teachers, find science in general (and chemistry in particular) mysterious and threatening. When given a chance, both teachers and students can enjoy transforming the classroom into a laboratory and exploring like real scientists. Consider being the catalyst for this transformation.

Unlike magicians, scientists attempt to find explanations for why and how things happen. Challenge students to join in on the fun of searching for explanations. At the introductory level, it is far more important to provide non-threatening opportunities for the students to postulate "why?" than it is for their responses to be absolutely complete. If the accepted explanation is too complex to discuss, maybe the emphasis of the presentation is wrong. For example, discussions focusing on the fact that a color change can be an indication of a chemical reaction may be more useful than a detailed explanation of the reaction mechanisms involved.

Because science involves the process of discovery, it is equally important to let the students know that not all the answers are known and that they too can make a difference. Teachers should be made to feel that responses like "I don't know. What do you think?" or "Let's find out together," are acceptable. It is also important to point out that not everyone's results will be the same. Reinforce the idea that a student's results are not wrong just because they are different from a classmate's results.

While using the term "chemistry," try relating the topics to real-life experiences and integrating topics into non-science areas. After all, chemistry is all around us, not just in the chemistry lab.

When interacting with students, take care to involve all of them. It is very worthwhile to spend time talking informally with small groups or individual students before, during, or after your presentation. It is important to convey the message that chemistry is for all who are willing to apply themselves to the questions before them. Chemistry is neither sexist, racist, nor frightening.

For more information on becoming involved in the classroom and a practical and valuable discussion of some do's and don'ts, a resource is available. The American Chemical Society Education Division has an informative booklet and video called *Chemists in the Classroom.* You may request this package for $20.00 from: ACS Education Division, American Chemical Society, 1155 Sixteenth Street NW, Washington, DC 20036, 800/227-5558.

How to Use This Teacher Resource Module

This section is an introduction to the Teacher Resource Module and its organization. The industry featured in this module is the food industry.

How Is This Resource Module Organized?

The Teacher Resource Module is organized into the following main sections: How to Use This Teacher Resource Module (this section), Background for Teachers, Using the Activities in the Classroom, and Activities and Demonstrations. Background for Teachers includes Overview of the Food Industry, Overview of Procter & Gamble, and Content Review. Using the Activities in the Classroom includes Pedagogical Strategies, an Annotated List of Activities and Demonstrations, and a Curriculum Placement Guide. The following paragraphs provide a brief overview of the *Science Fare—Chemistry at the Table* module.

Background for Teachers

Overviews of the food industry and Procter & Gamble's role in the industry provide information to help you feature the industrial focus of these activities in the classroom. The Content Review section is intended to provide you, the teacher, with an introduction to (or a review of) the concepts covered in the module. The material in this section (and in the individual activity explanations) intentionally gives you information at a level beyond what you will present to your students. You can then evaluate how to adjust the content presentation for your own students.

The Content Review section in this module covers the following topics:
- The Chemical Senses
- Fats and Oils

Using the Activities in the Classroom

The Pedagogical Strategies section is intended to provide ideas for effectively teaching a unit on the food industry. It suggests a variety of ways to incorporate the industry-based activities presented in the module into your curriculum. The Annotated List of Activities and Demonstrations and the Curriculum Placement Guide provide recommended grade levels, descriptions of the activities, and recommended placement of the activities within a typical curriculum.

Module Activities

Each module activity provides complete instructions for conducting the activity in your classroom. These activities have been classroom-tested by teachers like yourself and have been demonstrated to be practical, safe, and effective in the typical classroom. The following information is provided for each activity:

Recommended Grade Level:	The grade levels at which the activity will be most effective are listed.
Group Size:	The optimal student group size is listed.
Time for Preparation:	This includes time to set up for the activity before beginning with the students.

Time for Procedure:	This estimated time for conducting the activity is based on feedback from classroom testing, but your time may vary depending on your classroom and teaching style.
Materials:	Materials for each part of the activity are divided into amounts per class, per group, and per student.
Resources:	Sources for more difficult-to-find materials are listed.
Safety and Disposal:	Special safety and/or disposal procedures are listed if required. You should also closely read the Employing Appropriate Safety Procedures section of this teacher resource module.
Getting Ready:	Information is provided in Getting Ready when preparation is needed prior to beginning the activity with the students.
Opening Strategy:	A strategy for introducing the topic to be covered and for gaining the students' interest is suggested.
Procedure:	The steps in the Procedure are directed toward you, the teacher, and include cautions and suggestions where appropriate.
Variations and Extensions:	Variations are alternative methods for doing the Procedure. Extensions are methods for furthering student understanding.
Discussion:	Possible questions for students are provided, along with answers where appropriate.
Explanation:	The Explanation is written to you, the teacher, and is intended to be modified for students.
Key Science Concepts:	Targeted key science topics are listed.
Cross-Curricular Integration:	Cross-Curricular Integration provides suggestions for integrating the science activity with other areas of the curriculum.
References:	References used to write this activity are listed.

Notes and safety cautions are included in activities as needed and are indicated by the following icons and type style:

Notes are preceded by an arrow.

Cautions are preceded by an exclamation point.

Employing Appropriate Safety Procedures

Experiments, demonstrations, and hands-on activities add relevance, fun, and excitement to science education at any level. However, even the simplest activity can become dangerous when the proper safety precautions are ignored or when the activity is done incorrectly or performed by students without proper supervision. While the activities in this book include cautions, warnings, and safety reminders from sources believed to be reliable, and while the text has been extensively reviewed, it is your responsibility to develop and follow procedures for the safe execution of any activity you choose to do. You are also responsible for the safe handling, use, and disposal of chemicals in accordance with local and state regulations and requirements.

Safety First

- Collect and read the Materials Safety Data Sheets (MSDS) for all of the chemicals used in your experiments. MSDS's provide physical property data, toxicity information, and handling and disposal specifications for chemicals. They can be obtained upon request from manufacturers and distributors of these chemicals. In fact, MSDS's are often shipped with chemicals when they are ordered. These should be collected and made available to students, faculty, or parents for information about specific chemicals in these activities.

- Read and follow the American Chemical Society Minimum Safety Guidelines for Chemical Demonstrations on the next page. Remember that you are a role model for your students—your attention to safety will help them develop good safety habits while assuring that everyone has fun with these activities.

- Read each activity carefully and observe all safety precautions and disposal procedures. Determine and follow all local and state regulations and requirements.

- Never attempt an activity if you are unfamiliar or uncomfortable with the procedures or materials involved. Consult a high school or college chemistry teacher or an industrial chemist for advice or ask him or her to perform the activity for your class. These people are often delighted to help.

- Always practice activities yourself before using them with your class. This is the only way to become thoroughly familiar with an activity, and familiarity will help prevent potentially hazardous (or merely embarrassing) mishaps. In addition, you may find variations that will make the activity more meaningful to your students.

- Undertake activities only at the recommended grade levels and only with adult supervision.

- You, your assistants, and any students participating in the preparation for or doing of the activity must wear safety goggles if indicated in the activity and at any other time you deem necessary.

- Special safety instructions are not given for everyday classroom materials being used in a typical manner. Use common sense when working with hot, sharp, or breakable objects. Keep tables or desks covered to avoid stains. Keep spills cleaned up to avoid falls.

- When an activity requires students to smell a substance, instruct them to smell the substance as follows: hold its container approximately 6 inches from the nose and, using the free hand, gently waft the air above the open container toward the nose. Never smell an unknown substance by placing it directly under the nose. (See figure.)

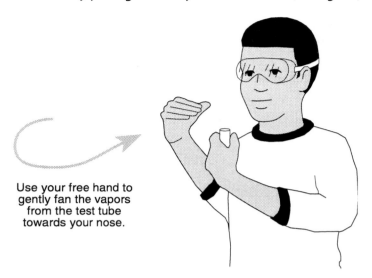

Use your free hand to gently fan the vapors from the test tube towards your nose.

Wafting procedure—Carefully wave the air above the open container towards your nose. Avoid hitting the container in the process.

- Caution students never to taste anything made in the laboratory and not to place their fingers in their mouths after handling laboratory chemicals.

ACS Minimum Safety Guidelines for Chemical Demonstrations

This section outlines safety procedures that Chemical Demonstrators must follow at all times.

1. Know the properties of the chemicals and the chemical reactions involved in all demonstrations presented.

2. Comply with all local rules and regulations.

3. Wear appropriate eye protection for all chemical demonstrations.

4. Warn the members of the audience to cover their ears whenever a loud noise is anticipated.

5. Plan the demonstration so that harmful quantities of noxious gases (e.g., NO_2, SO_2, H_2S) do not enter the local air supply.

6. Provide safety shield protection wherever there is the slightest possibility that a container, its fragments or its contents could be propelled with sufficient force to cause personal injury.

7. Arrange to have a fire extinguisher at hand whenever the slightest possibility for fire exists.

8. Do not taste or encourage spectators to taste any non-food substance.

9. Never use demonstrations in which parts of the human body are placed in danger (such as placing dry ice in the mouth or dipping hands into liquid nitrogen).

10. Do not use "open" containers of volatile, toxic substances (e.g., benzene, CCl_4, CS_2, formaldehyde) without adequate ventilation as provided by fume hoods.

11. Provide written procedure, hazard, and disposal information for each demonstration whenever the audience is encouraged to repeat the demonstration.

12. Arrange for appropriate waste containers for and subsequent disposal of materials harmful to the environment.

Background for Teachers

This Teacher Resource Module, developed as part of the *Partners for Terrific Science* program, provides you, the teacher, with a brief overview of the food industry, a summary of Procter & Gamble's role in this industry, a Content Review, a Using the Activities in the Classroom section, and a collection of activities and demonstrations.

Overview of the Food Industry

As you walk through a grocery store, many food options are available. Out of season, exotic and unusual foods are found in produce sections and in many aisles. A wide variety of packaged foods simplify food storage and preparation. Not too long ago, an orange was considered a rare treat at certain times of the year, a holiday gift to be treasured. Now we consider them common. Many foods that were once considered rare or seasonal are available to us year-round. Agricultural engineers and food chemists have perfected methods of protecting and shipping foods from far-off places, and as a result we can shop year-round for our favorite foods. This process always begins with raw materials from farmers, but tracing food from raw material to kitchen table involves many steps and many people. An acre of corn could be found processed in everything from chips to bread to soft drinks in the acres of aisles at your local grocery store.

The farmer, fisherman, or cattle rancher alone does not process the raw material to meet consumer needs. The food industry is responsible for the many steps in food processing. The food industry is one of the world's largest industries, and the fourth largest in America. About 10% of all industrial workers in the United States are employed in food manufacturing and processing. Food processing involves making raw resources suitable for cooking, consumption, and/or storage, qualities that we usually take for granted in the convenience food world we live in. Processing includes washing, sorting, preparing for safe storage, and manufacturing foods from basic plant and animal materials. The scope of this step is large and varied.

Food research is the continual effort to improve each aspect of food processing. Food company researchers work to develop new foods, make the home preparation of food easier, and enhance the nutritional content and safety of foods. Tasks such as enhancing the flavoring, speeding up the baking process, and making everyday foods healthier involve food chemistry, and food chemists work daily to improve the foods we eat in many ways. Chemists also test the foods we eat to ensure safe consumption and to make sure that nutrient levels meet federal regulations. Government regulations have control over every aspect of the food industry, including labeling, and the resulting information labels have been very beneficial to the consumer. Consumers can now make knowledgeable choices in the grocery store by reading labels.

Overview of Procter & Gamble

Based in Cincinnati, Ohio, Procter & Gamble is one of the largest global suppliers of consumer goods with sales for the 1993–1994 fiscal year exceeding $30 billion and net earnings totaling $2.2 billion. Procter & Gamble markets a broad range of food, laundry, cleaning, paper, beauty care, health care, and beverage products in more than 140 countries around the world. Among its highly recognized brands are Tide®, Dawn®, Pampers®, Crest®, Max Factor®, Vicks®, Crisco®, and Folgers®.

The Procter & Gamble World Headquarters in Cincinnati, Ohio

Procter & Gamble was founded in 1837, when William Procter, a candle maker, and James Gamble, a soap maker, joined forces to become business partners. They were brothers-in-law and, until their partnership, had competed with one another for the animal fats needed to produce each of their products.

Entry into the foods business came about as Procter & Gamble utilized experience in processing fats and oils to develop a replacement for lard (animal fat), which was becoming too costly to market. In 1910, Procter & Gamble patented Crisco shortening. A shortening is a blend of solid fat and liquid oil. Crisco was the first all-vegetable-based shortening and is made from soybean and cottonseed oils. The solid portion of the Crisco is made from hydrogenated soybean and cottonseed oils.

Hydrogenation is a process in which hydrogen is chemically added to unsaturated compounds such as oils, causing the liquid oil to solidify into a fat. Blending the vegetable oil and vegetable-based fat created a product that was not only economical to produce, but had an added advantage of a more stable shelf life than the pure oil.

Today, Procter & Gamble's food business markets a variety of products under such brand names as Crisco, Jif®, Duncan Hines®, and Pringles®. The success of each of these brands remains highly dependent upon the successful application and further development of the knowledge and experience with fats and oils that Procter & Gamble has gained throughout the years.

Some familiar Procter & Gamble products

Content Review

This section provides a basic overview of some of the more important and complex content areas to be addressed in the activities. We begin by discussing the senses of smell and taste. Then we will examine the chemistry of food. Food chemistry involves the study of the following important food groups: lipids (fats and oils), carbohydrates (starch and sugars), proteins, vitamins, and food additives (such as flavors and leavening agents). Because of the importance of lipids to the food industry, we will focus much of this discussion on these molecules. The other categories will be covered in less detail here or as needed in the laboratory activities.

The Chemical Senses

Several of the module activities explore flavors and odors—how they are produced by the food industry and perceived by the human senses.

The Sense of Smell

Smell, along with its partner, taste, are the chemical senses—the substances we smell or taste bond chemically to receptors in our noses or mouths. This process triggers a complex set of chemical reactions that culminate in the passage of an electric signal to the brain.

The act of smelling begins when air carries particles of a volatile substance into your nose. These particles are carried to the back of the nose, where about five million olfactory neurons (nerve cells devoted to smelling) wait in a bed of moist, mucus-bathed tissue. Each of the olfactory neurons is topped with eight or more hairlike cilia. These cilia contain odor receptors. The upper part of these odor receptors forms a pocket to hold odor molecules, and the lower part is embedded inside the cell. When an odor molecule floats into this area, it dissolves in the mucus around the cilia and is carried into the correctly-shaped receptor pocket. When the pocket takes in a molecule, the pocket twists slightly, releasing special proteins into the cell. These proteins interact with other proteins in the cell to open channels in the cell's membrane and allow electrically charged sodium ions to enter the cell. When the charge in the cell builds up to a certain level, the cell puts out an electric pulse, which passes up the neuron to one of the olfactory bulbs at the base of the brain. The olfactory bulb relays the signal to the part of the brain responsible for interpreting the signal.

The nose may contain as many as 1,000 different olfactory receptors, in contrast to the eye, which contains only three types of light receptors (those sensitive to red, green, or blue light). These thousand or so receptors are able to recognize about 10,000 distinct odors. This number difference suggests that each receptor may be able to recognize more than one smell, in which case the brain may need signals from more than one neuron to identify the smell, and thus may rely on some kind of code. If each neuron bears cilia carrying more than one type of receptor, the detection code may be very complicated.

Not everyone has equal smelling ability. More than two million Americans (about 1% of the population) suffer from significant loss of smelling ability. This condition, called anosmia, is often caused by a head injury, but can also be caused by a gene defect, aging, viral infections, allergies, or even prescription drugs (as a side effect). Often anosmia caused by head injuries heals on its own, but in some cases it becomes permanent.

The Sense of Taste

Taste, like smell, is a chemical sense. The substances we taste are chemicals (food molecules), and the method of sending signals to the brain is based on chemical reactions. The ability to sense chemicals may be the oldest sense, predating sight and the other senses by millions of years. Every organism, from single-celled bacteria to complex vertebrates like humans, senses chemicals. Chemical sensing in many organisms is essential to survival. Bacteria and many simple organisms rely on smell/taste to find food and avoid poisons.

Taste is one of the most commonly misunderstood senses. Much of what we usually think of as taste—that sense that allows us to savor our food and distinguish between fine wines—is really smell. When food enters our mouths, molecules of the substance waft up into our noses through the pharynx, a tunnel opening at the back of the mouth. (See Figure 1.)

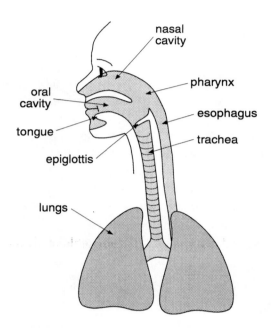

Figure 1: The pharynx connects the oral and nasal cavities.

Thus we can smell and taste simultaneously. Without the sense of smell, we would be unable to identify many foods we often think of as having distinct flavors. If you don't believe this statement, try eating several flavors of jelly beans one at a time while holding your nose. If you feel particularly doubtful, try eating a piece of apple and a piece of onion while holding your nose.

In all land vertebrates, the organs of taste, called taste buds, are located in the mouth. In humans, the taste buds are found on the tongue. Human taste buds distinguish between four major qualities: sweet, salty, sour, and bitter. (See Figure 2.) Some researchers also consider that monosodium glutamate (the flavor enhancer commonly called MSG) and related chemicals have a distinct taste. These four (or five) tastes may not seem very helpful when compared to the thousands of smells we can identify, but these tastes provide important basic information about the substances we put in our mouths. Sweetness is typical of high-energy foods. Saltiness can tell us if a food can restore sodium chlorides and potassium chlorides lost during exercise. Poisonous or spoiled food often tastes bitter, while unripe foods often taste sour. Cues like these help us steer toward good food and away from poisons and other harmful substances. The smell or sight of a food may not provide ample information to identify a type of food, so taste is an important last check before a substance goes "down the hatch."

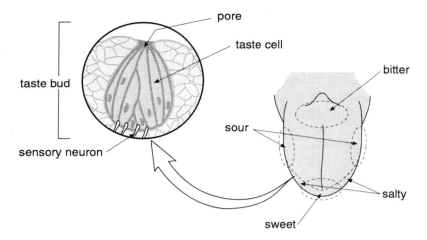

Figure 2: The structure of the taste buds and the areas of the tongue most sensitive to the four basic tastes

When a substance enters the mouth, particles of the substance are dissolved in saliva. These dissolved particles stimulate the taste buds. (See Figure 2.) Each taste bud is an onion-shaped organ consisting of a cluster of about 100 thin cells. These cells are not neurons (nerve cells), but they can send electrical signals and are sensitive to chemicals. The top ends of these cells are crowded together into a small pore in the tongue's surface. Particles of the dissolved substance entering the pore come in contact with these chemically sensitive cells, which send electrical pulses to neurons connected to them. These neurons then fire off taste messages to the brain.

Taste buds probably don't generate electrical pulses in the same way for every taste. For example, sweet and bitter particles stimulate taste cells by binding to special receptors at their tips. Researchers believe that special proteins from these receptors flow into the taste cells and start the chemical reactions that produce an electrical pulse. (These special proteins are believed to play a similar role in the sense of smell.) Salty and sour substances, however, probably bypass the receptors to excite the taste cells directly. Charged particles from salt (sodium ions) and the protons (hydrogen atoms with no electrons) that cause sourness pass through open ion channels at the tips of the cells of the taste buds. These ions probably generate the electrical pulse directly, without the use of the special proteins from the receptors.

Apparently, any taste bud can respond to three or even four tastes, but they are more sensitive to some than to others. The taste bud fires off a different code for each taste encountered.

Fats and Oils

Two activities in this collection, "The Densities of Fats and Oils" and "The Fat Content of Snack Food," require you to have some understanding of lipids. Lipids are a class of biological molecules that include fats, oils, steroids (such as cholesterol) and terpenes (such as vitamin A and carotene). (Figure 3 provides a mental picture of types of lipids.) Lipids can be divided into polar and nonpolar lipids. Polar lipids include the lipids in cell membranes and are generally not important for a discussion of foods. Nonpolar lipids are subdivided into saponifiable lipids (including fats and oils) and non-saponifiable lipids (such as steroids). Saponification is the reaction with a strong base to form soaps. ("Sapo" comes from a Latin word meaning "soap.")

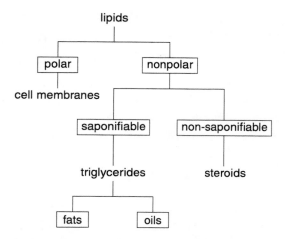

Figure 3: A diagram of different categories of lipids with examples

Fats and oils are the simplest and most abundant kinds of lipids. As previously noted, they belong to the nonpolar class of lipids that are saponifiable. While fats and oils are termed the simplest kinds of lipids, they often have large, complex structures which can be intimidating to beginning chemistry students.

Triglycerides

The basic molecules that make up fats and oils are called triglycerides. Triglycerides (also called triacylglycerols) are complex esters of glycerol and fatty acids. Esters contain the functional –COOR group, where R is a hydrocarbon chain, and are made by reacting a carboxylic acid (–COOH) with an alcohol (–OH). Figure 4 shows equations for both the general reaction (where R and R' are carbon chains) as well as a specific reaction that results in the formation of the ester, ethyl acetate.

a. general reaction:

$$R\!-\!\overset{\overset{\displaystyle O}{\|}}{C}\!-\!OH \ + \ HO\!-\!R' \ \rightleftharpoons \ R\!-\!\overset{\overset{\displaystyle O}{\|}}{C}\!-\!O\!-\!R' + H_2O$$

carboxylic acid   alcohol   ester

b. specific reaction:

$$CH_3\!-\!\overset{\overset{\displaystyle O}{\|}}{C}\!-\!OH \ + \ HO\!-\!CH_2CH_3 \ \rightleftharpoons \ CH_3\!-\!\overset{\overset{\displaystyle O}{\|}}{C}\!-\!O\!-\!CH_2CH_3 + H_2O$$

acetic acid   ethyl alcohol   ethyl acetate

Figure 4: A general and specific reaction of a carboxylic acid (acetic acid) and an alcohol (ethyl alcohol) to form an ester (ethyl acetate) and water

Triglycerides are made by reacting glycerol with three fatty acids to form three ester bonds. (See Figure 5.) Fatty acids are naturally occurring carboxylic acids. These are discussed in more detail in the next section.

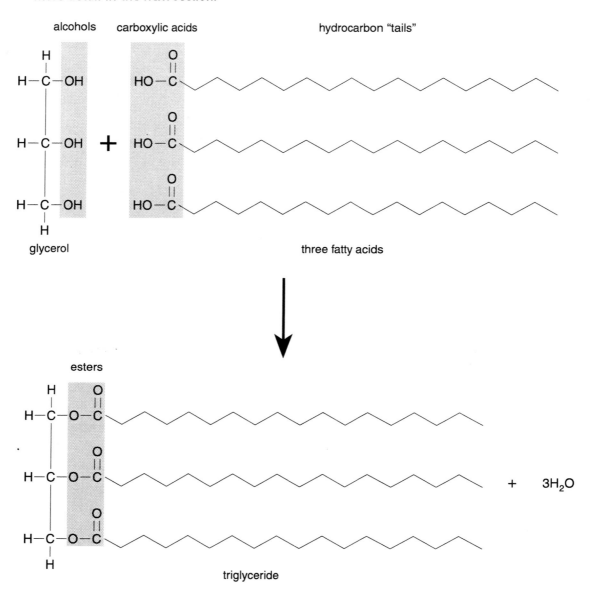

Figure 5: Glycerol combines with three fatty acids to produce a triglyceride and water.

Figure 6(a) shows two graphical representations of a simple triglyceride. Figure 6(b) shows the structural formula for one of the simple triglycerides.

a: simplified representations

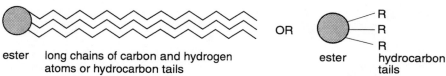

| ester | long chains of carbon and hydrogen atoms or hydrocarbon tails | | ester | hydrocarbon tails |

OR

b: structure

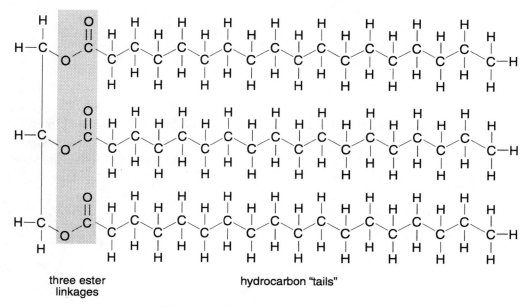

three ester linkages   hydrocarbon "tails"

Figure 6: A simple triglyceride

Fatty Acids

Fatty acids are the building blocks of triglycerides. Fatty acids are long-chain carboxylic acids (organic molecules that contain a –COOH group). Short-chain carboxylic acids such as acetic acid (See Figure 4) are not fatty acids.

The molecules of naturally occurring fatty acids have an even number of carbon atoms and have the carbons bonded sequentially with no carbon side-chains. While shorter-chain fatty acids do exist, the ones most commonly found in food sources have 16 or 18 carbons. Figure 7 shows the structures of three common fatty acids: 1) oleic acid, the 18-carbon fatty acid common in most oils; 2) stearic acid, the 18-carbon fatty acid common in fats such as beef tallow; and 3) palmitic acid, the 16-carbon fatty acid found in tropical oils such as palm oil. Stearic and palmitic acids are saturated fatty acids; they contain only carbon-carbon single bonds (C–C). Oleic acid, on the other hand, is an unsaturated fatty acid. It contains one carbon-carbon double bond (C=C). Fatty acids with two or more carbon-carbon double bonds in their structure are called polyunsaturated fatty acids.

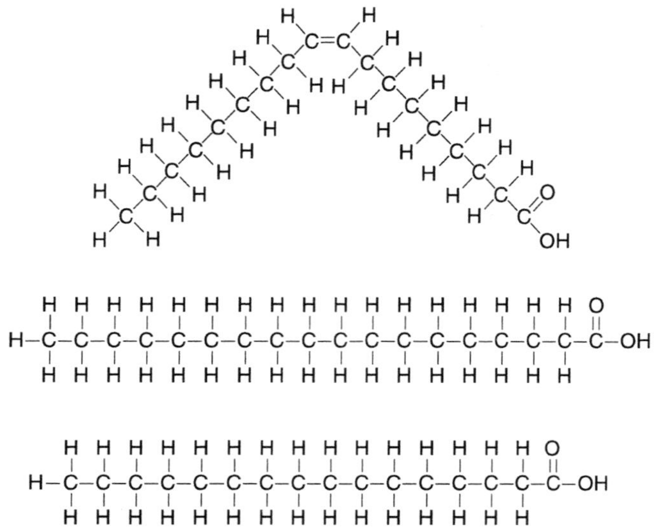

oleic acid
$C_9H_{18} = C_8H_{15}COOH$

stearic acid
$C_{17}H_{35}COOH$

palmitic acid
$C_{15}H_{31}COOH$

Figure 7: The structures of three common fatty acids

The carbon chains that are attached to the double bond have two possible geometric orientations. (See Figure 8.) In the cis (pronounced "sis") configuration, the carbon chains (represented by R and R') are attached to the same side of the double bond, causing it to appear bent like a block ⌐. Naturally occurring unsaturated fatty acids, including oleic acid (shown in Figure 7), are in the cis configuration. The other possible orientation for the carbon chains is called trans. The trans configuration places the carbon chains (again represented by R and R') on the opposite sides (or across) the double bond, giving the chain a stair-step orientation, ⌐.

cis

trans

Figure 8: Cis and trans configurations

Triglycerides: Oily Liquids or Waxy Solids

Triglycerides can be classified into two categories: simple and mixed. Simple triglycerides contain the same fatty acids in all three positions on the glycerol molecule (the R groups are all the same); mixed triglycerides contain two or more different fatty acids (the R groups are different). Natural fats are a mixture of simple and mixed triglycerides. Oleic acid makes up more than half of the total fatty acid content of most triglycerides.

Triglycerides can be waxy solids (called fats) or oily liquids (called oils). The determining factors are the relative number of saturated (contains C–C single bonds) versus unsaturated (contains C=C double bonds) fatty acids. Comparatively speaking, the greater the level of unsaturation (double bonds) in the triglyceride, the lower the melting point of the material and the greater the possibility it will be a liquid at room temperature. It should not be surprising to learn that vegetable oils (such as corn, olive, and canola oils) have high levels of unsaturated fatty acids and are liquid at room temperature. Animal fats (such as lard, tallow, and butter) have higher levels of saturated fatty acids (mostly single bonds), accounting for the fact that they are solid at room temperature.

The difference in melting points between saturated and unsaturated fatty acids can be explained by looking at their skeletal structures. The zigzag structure of saturated fatty acids allows them to pack tightly together, maximizing the interactions between the molecules. Such an arrangement accounts for the fact that triglycerides with high saturated fatty acid content tend to be solid, fats, at room temperature. The bent ⌐ orientation of the cis double bonds in unsaturated fatty acids prevents the triglyceride molecules from packing closely together, and so the interactions between the molecules are weak. (See Figure 9.) The weak interactions between the different triglyceride molecules result in unsaturated fats being liquids, oils, at room temperature.

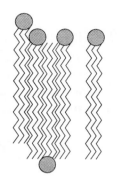

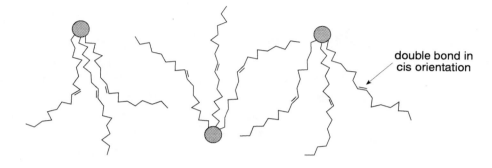

double bond in cis orientation

Fats: triglycerides with a high degree of saturation

Oils: triglycerides with a high degree of unsaturation

Figure 9: A graphical representation of the packing of saturated and unsaturated triglycerides

Chain length also affects the state a triglyceride is in at room temperature. Palm and coconut oils, while highly saturated, are liquids at room temperature because they are made of relatively short-chain fatty acids.

Reactions of Fatty Acids

Hydrogenation: Unsaturated fats (those that contain C=C bonds) can be made more saturated by a chemical process called hydrogenation. (See Figure 10.) Hydrogenation converts double bonds (C=C) to single bonds (C–C) by adding hydrogens to the double bonds. When unsaturated oils become hydrogenated, they typically become solid due to the packing of the chains that is possible in saturated systems. (See previous section.)

$$\underset{R}{\overset{H}{\underset{|}{C}}}=\underset{R'}{\overset{H}{\underset{|}{C}}} \quad + \quad H_2 \quad \longrightarrow \quad H-\underset{R}{\overset{H}{\underset{|}{C}}}-\underset{R'}{\overset{H}{\underset{|}{C}}}-H$$

Figure 10: The general reaction for the hydrogenation process

In addition to reducing the level of saturation in an oil, the process of hydrogenation can cause a secondary (or side) reaction that causes cis double bonds to be converted to trans double bonds. The stair-step orientation of trans double bonds allows them to align more easily at room temperature than their cis precursors and accounts for their existing as solids at room temperature. Trans fatty acids are not naturally occurring and exist in fats and oils only as a result of this reaction.

The food industry has done many studies to make sure that trans fatty acids are safe for humans. Recent studies in the U.S. and the Netherlands revealed that consumption of significant quantities of foods containing trans fatty acids causes both an increase in the serum cholesterol level and an increase in the levels of harmful LDL (low density lipoproteins). There was an associated decrease in the levels of beneficial HDL (high density lipoproteins). LDLs are associated with atherosclerosis, while HDLs have been shown to protect against heart disease. This double effect (raising both serum cholesterol and LDL levels) has researchers concerned about the consumption of trans fatty acids. While more studies are being conducted, it is recommended that vegetable oils be used for cooking. Soft margarine or spread might be used for baking with special recipes. (Margarine, by law, must be 80% fat, making it interchangeable with butter for older recipes.)

Rancidity: With time, fats and oils become rancid due to a series of chemical reactions that cause the molecules to decompose into smaller molecules, some of which have unpleasant tastes and odors. (For example, butyric acid is responsible for the odor of rancid butter.) The rancidity process typically begins with a hydrolysis process that involves the addition of water to a triglyceride. (See Figure 11.) This hydrolysis reaction is accelerated by an enzyme produced by microorganisms in the air and is the reverse of the esterification reaction shown in Figure 4. Glycerol and fatty acids are the products of this hydrolysis reaction. Fats can also become rancid by reacting with oxygen in the air.

The fatty acids formed by the hydrolysis reaction can be further decomposed as a result of oxidation reactions that are catalyzed by an enzyme in the food. (These oxidation reactions produce molecules such as small-chain aldehydes and organic acids.) Oxidation reactions can be retarded by adding antioxidants such as vitamin C (ascorbic acid), vitamin E (α-tocopherol), BHA (butylated hydroxyanisole), or BHT (butylated hydroxytoluene) to products or by refrigerating the fat or oil. These chemicals defer oxidation of the fatty acid in that they are preferentially oxidized in place of the fatty acid. Refrigerating (or cooling) the fat or oil helps slow both the oxidation and hydrolysis reactions.

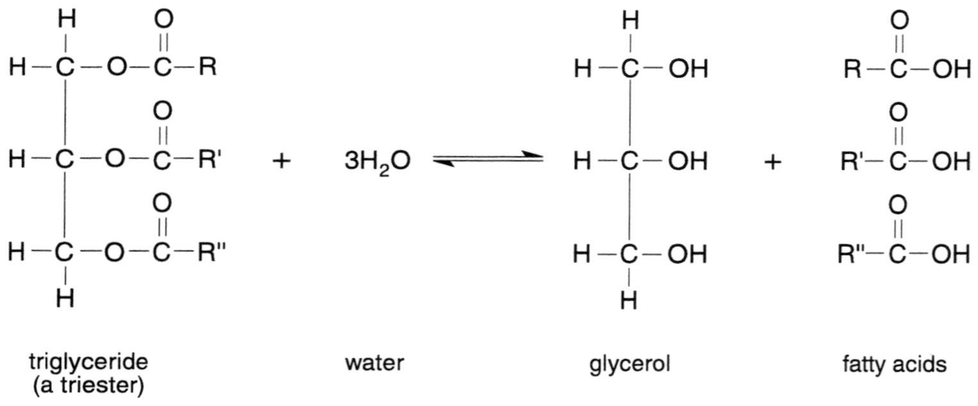

Figure 11: Hydrolysis of a triglyceride

Saponification: The chemistry of making soap involves hydrolizing a triglyceride (fat) with a strong base such as sodium hydroxide (NaOH). The reaction, called saponification, is shown in Figure 12. Soaps are sodium, potassium, or sometimes ammonium salts of fatty acids.

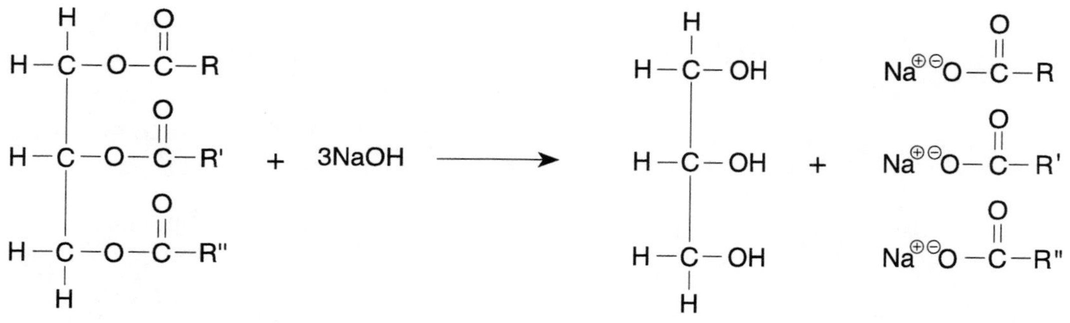

Figure 12: The saponification reaction of a triglyceride

Cholesterol

While cholesterol is not a triglyceride, it is a naturally occurring lipid which has come under close scrutiny because of its link to atherosclerosis. Its structure is shown in Figure 13. It is a nonpolar lipid which does not undergo saponification reactions because it does not contain ester or other bonds which react in this manner.

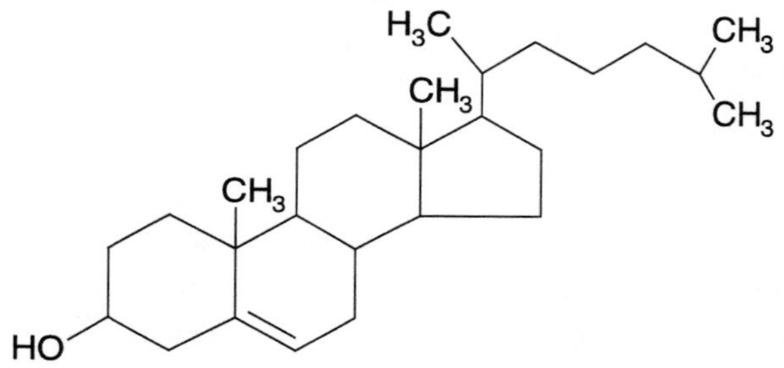

Figure 13: The structure of cholesterol

Cholesterol is produced naturally from saturated fatty acids by animals including humans, but not by plants. This is one reason why nutritionists recommend a diet low in saturated fats.

Lipids and Nutrition

Nutritionists recommend that adults limit their fat intake to 30% of the total calories ingested. Unfortunately, the typical American diet derives nearly 40% of its calories from fat. In general, snack food, fast food, and convenience foods get 40% or more of their calories from fat. Foods that are high in fat include potato chips, French fries, bacon, corn chips, peanut butter, nuts, chocolate, and frozen dinners. Even popcorn is considered to be high in fat if it is cooked in oil. Most microwave popcorn is especially high in fat; 50–60% of its calories comes from fat. It is important for consumers to be aware of how much fat foods contain in order to control their fat intake. Many fast food restaurants provide nutrition information about their products. Convenience foods have the information on the label.

It has been known for many years that a diet high in fat and cholesterol can lead to atherosclerosis and heart disease. Over the past 40 years, Americans have made a concerted effort to change their diets by substituting polyunsaturated fats found in vegetables for saturated fats and cholesterol. This change in diet has contributed to a 40% decrease in the number of deaths due to heart disease since 1950. Although this statistic is impressive, scientists have continued to search for other dietary changes to further reduce the risk of heart disease. Research has shown that groups of people whose diets consisted mainly of fish and seafood experienced much lower instances of death due to heart disease. Although fish and seafood are high in fat, the fat in fish contains polyunsaturated fatty acids similar to those found in vegetables. People eating fish were found to experience much lower instances of blood clotting and plaque formation within the blood vessels.

Vitamins are organic molecules that are essential to maintaining body health. These important molecules, however, are not synthesized by the body in amounts sufficient for its needs. Thus, vitamins must be a regular part of the diet for proper cellular function, growth, and reproduction. Most people who eat a balanced diet obtain the Recommended Dietary Allowance (RDA) without taking vitamin supplements.

Vitamins can be classified into two main groups on the basis of their solubility. The first group of vitamins are water-soluble, which means they will dissolve in water. Water-soluble vitamins include all the B vitamins (such as thiamin, niacin, riboflavin, B_6, and B_{12}) and vitamin C. The second group of vitamins are fat-soluble, which means they do not dissolve in water, but instead in fats and oils. The fat-soluble vitamins include vitamins A, D, E, and K. Activity 10, "Solubility of Vitamins," builds upon the understanding of fats gained in Activities 1 and 2, since students classify vitamins as fat- or water-soluble.

Water-soluble vitamins are soluble in the blood (which is mostly water). Once in the blood, water-soluble vitamins end up in the kidneys where excess amounts of the vitamins are excreted in the urine. Since water-soluble vitamins are not stored in the body, they must be present in the daily diet. It is important to take in the RDA of these vitamins each day. Fruits and vegetables are very good sources of the water-soluble vitamins.

In contrast, fat-soluble vitamins can be stored in body fat. Because any excess of the fat-soluble vitamins is stored, ingestion of large doses of these vitamins can be toxic. When ingesting fat-soluble vitamins, too much can be just as harmful as too little. People who take large doses of fat-soluble vitamins can develop a disease called "hypervitaminosis." This is a toxic reaction that results from the buildup of fat-soluble vitamins. For example, an excess of vitamin A (7.5 mg per day for 25 days) results in an increase in spinal fluid, headaches, irritability, patchy loss of hair, dry skin with sores, and eventually an orange cast to the skin.

Using the Activities in the Classroom

The activities in this module help students become aware of the importance of the food industry. As they experiment with properties that determine the quality, appearance, taste, texture, and smell of foods, they learn the role of chemistry and technology in designing food products which are appealing, stable, and healthy for consumers.

Pedagogical Strategies

When introducing this module, you may wish to discuss how odor, taste, touch, and sight are used to give people their perception and preferences for specific food types. Smell and taste together give us our impression of flavor. The sense of touch gives us an impression of a food's texture and temperature. Sight plays a role in our final perception of food. A food's color and appearance are important to its appeal.

Learning Cycle

Using the activities "Sense-Fooling Pies," "Flavors Are Chemicals," and "Esters Are Food Flavorings," a learning cycle can be created in which students are challenged to investigate their perceptions concerning what makes a given food appealing.

The first phase of the cycle, "Sense-Fooling Pies," challenges students' preconceived notions about food, especially taste, by presenting them with a discrepant event. Prepare a No-Apple Apple Pie from the recipe in "Sense-Fooling Pies" and ask students to taste and identify the type of pie. After the students have identified the pie as apple, list the pie's ingredients on the board. Students will be surprised that there are no apples in the pie and learn that taste is a response to certain chemicals or groups of chemicals.

The second phase of the cycle allows students to make observations and collect data while confronting their preconceived notions. The activity "Flavors Are Chemicals" allows students to identify flavors by aroma. By doing the variations in the activity and allowing students to taste food flavorings with noses first closed and then open, students will recognize the interaction of the senses of taste and smell.

The final phase helps students explore and form new conceptions based upon their observations and data as well as apply their knowledge and understanding in a new hands-on activity. In "Esters Are Food Flavorings," students synthesize various food flavorings known as esters. Students learn that esters are formed in a process called esterification when carboxylic acids are reacted with an alcohol.

Cooperative Learning

Have students form consumer-testing groups for a given food-related industry. Students could prepare test food samples (which vary in use of natural and artificial flavorings, types of leavening agents, or types of fats) to be sampled by consumers. The consumers could be students from another classroom. (Note: All food samples should be prepared at home or in a home economics room under proper adult supervision.) The students could prepare survey sheets on which consumers record their preferences for or their ability to distinguish between given food types.

Science-Technology-Society

Students can research the steps needed to produce a given food product. Have students start with food source production and follow that source through all the manufacturing and packaging processes needed to put the chosen product on grocery store shelves. Students can determine the cost of producing the product, the safety and handling concerns associated with the product, as well as the regulations that must be followed in the manufacture and marketing of the product. (The amount of detail included in this report would vary greatly with the ability and grade level of the students.)

Examine some of the types of packaging necessary for different kinds of food products. Discuss the topic of recycling and disposal of the packages. List properties of the different types of materials which are necessary to preserve and protect different types of foods.

Cross-Curricular Strategies

- Health classes that discuss the five senses may do a unit on how the senses are important in evaluating food products. Elementary students can make "feel boxes" in which substances with different textures are placed in a box so the substance cannot be seen. Students reach into the box and try to describe the texture. Substances could include cotton, sandpaper, gelatin, plastic, etc. The sense of smell can be illustrated with various food flavors (as in "Esters Are Food Flavorings"). Taste tests can be done with different fruit drinks. These may be colored with food color to see if the appearance influences the perception of the flavor. Food products such as peanut butter, cakes, cookies, popcorn, or potato chips may be studied to see how the color, odor, texture, and taste are all important in determining what products are appealing to consumers.

- Biology or nutrition classes might examine the storage of foods in various containers and at different temperatures to determine the effect on product stability. Students can also research how saturated and unsaturated fats and/or water-soluble and fat-soluble vitamins affect the human body.

- Mathematics classes can be involved in measurements of density of different food products. They can also do statistical analyses of data collected by surveys to determine various preferences. Students should design the necessary parameters for the survey in advance and decide on the best way of collecting data. Students can conduct their own "taste tests" of products to see which ones are preferred. Results can then be analyzed and presented by different graphical methods.

- Students in art classes can design a label for a new product prepared by the class. They will need to do research about which features would be most likely to get consumers to buy the product. Different types of labels can be made to appeal to different groups of consumers: children, adults, athletes, etc.

- Social studies classes can list the number of different types of vegetable oils that are sold in a grocery. Then they can carry out a library research project to determine where in the United States and other countries the different types of oil-producing plants are grown.

  Have students research the current world food supply and availability. Find out the impact modern farming techniques have had on food production as well as the impact they have had on the environment.

- Strengthen students' oral and written communication skills by requiring presentations, written lab reports, and/or a lab journal.

Individual and Group Projects

- Develop a recipe for a new fruit-flavored cereal. Determine which flavorings to use as well as the types and amounts of minerals and vitamins to include.

- List the various flavors of cake mixes available at a grocery. Survey friends to determine preferences among the various flavors. Analyze the data and report it graphically.

- Do library research on the development of peanuts as a food product in the United States. In the grocery, find a number of different food products which contain peanuts. Examine the economic value of peanuts as a food crop.

- Do library research on the fatty acids present in the human body and the proportions in which they are present. Draw the molecular structures of these fatty acids.

- Make a molecular model of a triglyceride that can be found in the human body. Use gumdrops and toothpicks for the atoms and bonds, or use small Styrofoam™ balls and pipe cleaners to hold the balls together.

- Make molecular models of cis and trans fatty acids. Show how the molecules "stack" differently when they come together as they do in the solid phase.

- Make a "wave bottle" by half-filling a plastic bottle with a liquid such as baby or vegetable oil and using water to fill the rest of the bottle. Color one of the liquids with food coloring. Measure the densities of each liquid (as in "The Densities of Fats and Oils") and use the density values to explain the relative positions of the liquids in the bottle.

- Study the label of a food product. Try to find out what each ingredient's purpose in that product is.

- Keep a log of all of the prepared food products (foods that were purchased in a box, can, plastic container, etc.) that are consumed during a one-week period.

A Classroom Company

Form a classroom company to design a food product, test it, and market it to other classes. The food product might be a type of cookie, cake, peanut butter, pie, candy, fruit drink, snack food, or "health" food. Students must first research the ingredients needed and decide which types of ingredients to try. They must prepare the product, experimenting with conditions such as baking time and temperature, quantity and types of ingredients, and procedures for preparation and packaging. They must devise an evaluation process to test different attributes of the process and answer questions such as, "Which color is most appealing?" "Which flavor do people prefer?" "Should the texture be light or heavy, smooth or chunky?"

Next, develop a marketing campaign. What should the product be named? What types of advertising should be used? What are the costs of producing the product? What would be a fair price for it?

Finally, prepare and market the product. Analyze the different strategies to determine which are most successful.

Annotated List of Activities and Demonstrations

To aid you in choosing activities for your classroom, we have included an annotated list of activities and demonstrations. This listing includes information about the grade level that can benefit most from an activity and a brief description of each activity. A Curriculum Placement Guide follows this list.

1. **Flavors Are Chemicals** (elementary to middle school)
   Students identify flavors by their aroma. A table of chemical ingredients for each flavor is included.

2. **A Vanilla Taste Test** (elementary to middle school)
   This activity describes a simple taste test to see if people really can taste the difference between natural and artificial vanilla.

3. **Sense-Fooling Pies** (elementary to high school)
   Ever tried to make an apple pie without apples? In this activity, alternative ingredients are substituted for apples, pecans, and bananas to make no-apple, no-pecan, or no-banana pies that could easily pass for the "real" things. Students discover the roles that aroma, texture, and appearance play in the sense of taste.

4. **Esters Are Food Flavorings** (upper elementary to high school)
   In this activity, various food flavorings known as esters are synthesized.

5. **Why Popcorn Pops** (upper elementary to high school)
   The first half of the activity is a teacher demonstration that shows the importance of moisture content in popcorn. The second half is a student activity in which they compare the volume of popped popcorn yielded for several brands of popcorn and calculate the percentage of water for each brand.

6. **Chemicals Make the Cake** (upper elementary to high school)
   Students bake cakes with different recipes to observe how the physical characteristics of an everyday item (in this case a cake) are determined by the chemicals from which it is made.

7. **The Action of Leavening Agents** (upper elementary to high school)
   Students test the amount of gas produced by common leavening agents including baking soda, baking powder, and yeast.

8. **The Densities of Fats and Oils** (upper elementary to high school)
   Students determine the numerical values for the densities of common household substances such as corn syrup, rubbing alcohol, vegetable oil, water, and butter.

9. **The Fat Content of Snack Food** (high school)
   Students extract the fat from a sample of snack food using hexane, an organic solvent, and calculate the percentage of fat found in the sample. Extensions involve comparing results for regular versus "lite" snacks.

10. **Solubility of Vitamins** (upper elementary to high school)
    Students test the solubility of vitamins A, E, and C in water and vegetable oil, and explore the implications of this solubility on toxicity and the need for a balanced diet.

Curriculum Placement Guide

Activities	Topics					
	Nature of Matter	Science and Technology	Scientific Method	Health	Mass, Volume, and Density	Chemical Reactivity
1 Flavors Are Chemicals	●	●	●			
2 A Vanilla Taste Test	●	●	●		●	●
3 Sense-Fooling Pies	●	●	●		●	●
4 Esters Are Food Flavorings	●	●	●		●	●
5 Why Popcorn Pops	●	●	●		●	●
6 Chemicals Make the Cake	●	●	●		●	●
7 The Action of Leavening Agents	●	●	●		●	●
8 The Densities of Fats and Oils	●	●	●	●	●	
9 The Fat Content of Snack Food	●	●	●	●	●	●
10 Solubility of Vitamins	●	●	●	●	●	

Activities and Demonstrations

Flavors Are Chemicals

Did you know that flavors are chemicals? In fact, most flavors (both natural and synthetic) are mixtures of many different chemicals. Flavors of food are perceived through a combination of taste and smell. In this activity, students determine the identities of several different flavors using only their sense of smell.

> **Recommended Grade Level** 1–8
> **Group Size** .... 1–4 students
> **Time for Preparation** .... 10 minutes
> **Time for Procedure** .... 20 minutes

Materials

Opening Strategy
- scratch-and-sniff stickers in a variety of colors

Procedure
Per Group
- 2 mL of 3 or more of the following food flavorings:
  - orange
  - anise
  - banana
  - cherry
  - pineapple
  - lemon
  - almond
  - coconut
  - vanilla
- small zipper-type plastic bag or 35-mm film canister for each flavoring
- cotton ball for each flavoring
- (optional) food color
- labels
- markers

Variations
- 1 of the following:
  - flavorings listed for the Procedure in unmarked containers and plastic toothpicks
  - gourmet jelly beans

Safety and Disposal

Instruct students to smell the different flavors using the wafting procedure described in Employing Appropriate Safety Procedures.

Caution students never to taste anything made in the laboratory and not to place their fingers in their mouths after handling reagent chemicals. Like all chemicals, flavorings can be toxic if ingested in large amounts.

Getting Ready

Prepare a set of bags or canisters for each group or a set for the class to share. Label the bags or canisters with a number or letter code. Place a small amount of each flavor (5–10 drops) on a cotton ball and place it in a plastic bag or canister, keeping a key that indicates where each flavor is located. If the color of the flavoring would give the answer to the students, you may want to add a small amount of food color to the cotton ball to hide the natural color of the flavoring. Once the cotton balls have been placed in the plastic bags or canisters, keep them closed to minimize students' pre-exposure to the odors.

Opening Strategy

Distribute a variety of scratch-and-sniff stickers to the students. Have them scratch the surfaces of the stickers and smell the scents that are released. Have a few students identify the scent of their sticker for the class. Explain to the students that there are chemicals on the stickers that cause the odors that they smell. These "smelly" chemicals can be used in other products for flavoring as well. Demonstrate the proper technique for using wafting to smell an unknown substance. (See Employing Appropriate Safety Procedures.)

Procedure

 Do not place the unknown substances in Step 1 directly under the nose to smell them.

1. Open one of the plastic bags or film canisters and gently waft the odor to your nose.

2. Identify the flavoring by its scent, reclose the bag or canister, and record your observation.

3. Repeat Steps 1 and 2 for the remaining flavorings.

4. Compare your observations with the answer key.

Variations

- Prepare bags or canisters that contain more than one flavoring and see if the students can identify the components.

- Experiment to see how much the sense of smell determines the flavor of food. Have the students taste the flavorings used in the activity or jelly beans representing the flavors from the activity. If using the flavorings, have the students dip a plastic toothpick into an extract and taste. Use a fresh toothpick for each test. Have them identify the flavors once with their noses closed, and again with their noses open.

Extension

- Have older students conduct library research on the chemistry of the different flavors. One resource that lists the structure, toxicity, and other interesting information about these chemicals is *The Merck Index*.

Discussion

- Ask students how the manufacturer got the scent on the scratch-and-sniff stickers. *The stickers are made by fastening microscopic capsules of the different chemicals on the surface of the sticker. When the student scratches the surface of the sticker, the capsules are broken and the scent is released.*

Explanation

Many of the flavorings used in this activity are made of a mixture of chemicals to achieve the desired taste and smell. The components of each flavor are listed in Table 1 at the end of this activity.

Most of what we perceive as the flavor of food is actually its aroma. Some of the more volatile molecules (those easily changed to a gas) travel directly into the nose and produce a characteristic smell before food enters the mouth. Other volatile molecules from the food travel to the nose through a path from the mouth up the back of the throat (pharynx) and into the nasal cavity. The odor-producing molecules attach to the receptor cells in the nose which set off a series of chemical reactions that send messages to the brain for interpretation.

The tongue's contribution to perceiving flavor is limited to the four basic tastes: sweet, sour, bitter, and salty. Once the taste buds detect the food, the associated sensory neurons send messages to the brain for interpretation. Smell and taste together provide us with a fairly vivid impression of the flavor of food. See the Content Review for a detailed discussion of the senses of taste and smell.

A good activity to show that flavor is a combination of smell and taste is to eat something like gourmet jelly beans with your nose closed and then with your nose open. When the nasal passage is closed, the jelly beans taste sweet. This is due to the fact that not only are the nostrils closed, preventing smells from being detected, but also smells are prevented from traveling through the pharynx into the nasal cavity. With your nose open, the different flavors of the jelly beans are recognized readily.

Key Science Concepts

- senses
- volatile molecules

Cross-Curricular Integration

Home, Safety, and Career
Discuss why flavors and spices are added to food.

Language Arts
Have students read books about the five senses and write papers describing how taste and smell help us taste food.

References

Farrell, K.T. *Spices, Condiments and Seasonings;* AVI: Westport, CT, 1985.

Freedman, D.H. "In the Realm of the Chemical," *Discover.* June 1993, Vol. 14(6), 69–76.

Fenaroli, G. *Fenaroli's Handbook of Flavor Ingredients,* 3rd ed.; The Chemical Rubber Company: Cleveland, OH, 1995.

Heath, H.B. *Flavor Technology: Profiles, Products, Applications;* AVI: Westport, CN, 1978.

The Merck Index, An Encyclopedia of Chemicals, Drugs, and Biologicals; Merck: Rahway, NJ, 1983.

Merory, J. *Food Flavorings: Composition, Manufacture and Use;* AVI: Westport, CT, 1968.

Table 1: The Major Components of Nine Flavors

Flavoring	Chemical Components	Notes About the Flavors
Orange Oil	limonene, n-decylic aldehyde, citral, linalool, isoprene, 3-methyl-1-butene	—
Anise Extract	80–90% anethole, a-pinene, methyl chavicol, p-methoxyphenlactone (anisketone), anisaldehyde	Artificial anise is often made from 100% anethole.
Banana	mostly isoamyl acetate	Isoamyl acetate is also known as banana oil.
Cherry	anisyl acetate, benzaldehyde, benzyl acetate, cinnamaldehyde, ethyl butyrate, ethyl oenanthate, tolualdehyde, vanillin, amyl butyrate, eugenol, anisic aldehyde, palmital	Other recipes for this flavoring exist, some of which contain even more components than this recipe.
Pineapple	mostly ethyl butyrate	Other recipes are available.
Lemon Oil	citral, citronella, limonene, linalool, α-pinene β-ocimene, terpen-4-ol, α-terpineol, geranyl acetate	The citral, citronella, linalool, limonene, and geranyl acetate appear to be the major lemon flavor ingredients.
Almond Extract	benzaldehyde, phenoxyacetonitrile	Almond-flavored liqueurs such as Amaretto were originally made from crushed apricot pits, which contained hydrogen cyanide (HCN). HCN is very poisonous. Its natural presence in almond pits creates a natural toxicity of items made from them. This was responsible for the laetrile poisonings in the late 1970s and early 1980s. In making the liqueur, the HCN gas escapes during processing. The almond extract used as a food flavoring has had the HCN removed.
Coconut	amyl formate, benzaldehyde, butyric acid, caproic acid, 4,4-dibutylbutyrolactone, ethyl acetate, ethyl heptylate, ethyl undecanoate, ethyl vanillin, methyl undecyl ketone, methyl nonanoate, γ-octalactone, vanillin	—
Vanilla	vanillin and ethyl vanillin	Ethyl vanillin is not found in natural vanilla. It is used in synthetic vanilla because it has a vanilla-like taste, but its taste is five times stronger than natural vanilla. Ethyl vanillin has an unpleasant taste in high concentrations. In imitation vanilla, ethyl vanillin is generally used in concentrations of 10% or less.

A Vanilla Taste Test

Are there really any differences between natural and artificial flavorings? Why do manufacturers make a big deal about using natural flavorings in their products? This activity describes a simple taste test that you can do to see if people really can taste the difference between natural and artificial vanilla.

Recommended Grade Level 3–8
Group Size .... 1–4 students
Time for Preparation .... 10–15 minutes
Time for Procedure .... 10 minutes

Materials

Per Class
- ⅔ cup sweetened condensed milk
- 4½ cups confectioner's sugar
- real vanilla extract
- imitation vanilla flavor
- saltine crackers
- large mixing bowl
- wooden spoon or hand mixer
- measuring cups
- measuring spoons
- 2 serving plates
- markers and labels

Safety and Disposal

Do not prepare food or eat in a laboratory and do not use laboratory glassware for mixing materials that are to be eaten.

Getting Ready

Because this food will be eaten by the students, be sure not to use laboratory glassware in the preparation. Prepare the imitation flavor and real vanilla extract mixtures outside of class so the students will not know which is real and which is imitation.

1. Measure ⅔ cup (half a can) sweetened condensed milk into a mixing bowl.

2. Gradually add 4½ cups confectioner's sugar and mix well. The mixture should be crumbly.

3. Separate the crumbly mixture into two batches.

4. Add ½ tsp real vanilla extract to one batch. Mix well. This is batch A.

5. Add ½ tsp imitation vanilla flavor to the other batch. Mix well. This is batch B.

6. Shape the mixture into small balls about the size of marbles. Keep the two batches separate.

7. Put each batch on a plate. Label the trays A and B. Put crackers on the plates so the students can cleanse their palates between samples.

Opening Strategy

Present the students with labels of products that are marked real versus imitation flavor (e.g., strawberry jam versus strawberry gum). Ask students who have tasted these products whether they could distinguish between real and imitation flavors.

Procedure

 This activity involves eating. It should not be done in a laboratory.

1. Taste a sample from Tray A. Chew it thoroughly and record how strong the vanilla flavor tastes according to this scale:
   1=very strong
   2=moderately strong
   3=mild
   4=weak
   5=no vanilla taste

2. Eat a cracker to clear the taste of sample A from your mouth.

3. Taste a sample from Tray B. Chew it thoroughly and record how strong the vanilla flavor tastes according to the scale in Step 1.

4. Eat a cracker to clear the taste of sample B from your mouth.

Discussion

- Ask students what differences they tasted between the two batches.
  Batch B had a much stronger taste than batch A.

Explanation

The major component of real vanilla extract is the chemical vanillin. Vanillin has an aroma very similar to pure vanilla. Its chemical structure is shown in Figure 1.

$$OH$$
$$OCH_3$$
$$C-H$$
$$O$$

Figure 1: The structure of vanillin

Real vanilla extract contains well over 100 other chemicals besides vanillin and is made by soaking cured vanilla beans in ethyl alcohol. The chemicals that produce the vanilla flavor are extracted into the alcohol, and this extract is allowed to age. During aging, the alcohol reacts with the chemicals in the extract. Some chemicals are broken down and others are joined together, giving vanilla extract its subtle flavor and characteristic odor.

Imitation vanilla flavoring, on the other hand, is made from very few chemicals. Sometimes only vanillin is used. Sometimes vanillin and ethyl vanillin are used. Ethyl vanillin is not found in vanilla plants. It has a taste very similar to vanillin but about five times stronger. Because of its potency, large amounts of it do not taste very good. It is very similar in chemical structure to vanillin, with the $-OCH_3$ replaced by $-OCH_2CH_3$.

Many people can taste the difference between imitation vanilla flavoring and real vanilla extract. This is because they notice the taste of the other chemicals in real vanilla or because the taste of the imitation vanilla is too strong.

Key Science Concepts

- chemistry of flavors
- extracts
- sense of taste

Cross-Curricular Integration

Social Studies

Have students research the history of vanilla cultivation. You may want to assign different phases in this history to different students. Some of the phases are outlined here:

- The Totonaco Indians of Mexico were the first people to cultivate vanilla.

- For hundreds of years people tried to grow vanilla outside Mexico. While the plant would grow, it would not produce beans.

- In 1836, a botanist named Charles Morren discovered that the vanilla flower could not pollinate itself and that most insects could not help pollinate it because of its shape. In Mexico a small bee unique to that country helped to pollinate the vanilla orchids. Morren pollinated the orchids by hand and they produced fruit.

- About five years later, a former slave named Edmond Albins discovered a much easier and more practical way to pollinate the flowers.

References

Farrell, K.T. *Spices, Condiments and Seasonings;* AVI: Westport, CN, 1985.

Fenaroli, G. *Fenaroli's Handbook of Flavor Ingredients,* 3rd ed.; Chemical Rubber Company: Cleveland, OH, 1995.

Heath, H.B. *Flavor Technology: Profiles, Products, Applications;* AVI: Westport, CN, 1978.

Merory, J. *Food Flavorings: Composition, Manufacture and Use;* AVI: Westport, CN, 1968.

Sense-Fooling Pies

The scientists and engineers at Procter & Gamble are often faced with the challenge of improving the flavor of a food product or finding an ingredient that will give a food product a certain flavor or texture. This activity shows students that different ingredients can be used to simulate the flavor and texture of familiar foods.

Recommended Grade Level 3–12
Group Size .... 1–4 students
Time for Preparation .... 15 minutes
Time for Procedure .... 75 minutes

Materials

Procedure
Per student
- dish
- eating utensil

Per class
- materials listed for 1 or more of the following pies:

No-Apple Apple Pie
- 2 9-in pre-made refrigerator pie crusts
- 25 Ritz® crackers
- 1½ cups sugar
- 1½ tsp cream of tartar
- 2 cups water
- 1 tsp cinnamon
- 1 tsp butter or margarine
- measuring cups and spoons
- 9-in pie plate
- large saucepan
- small saucepan for melting butter
- wooden spoon
- access to a stove
- knife

No-Pecan Pecan Pie
- 9-in pre-made refrigerator pie crust
- 1½ cups sugar
- 1 stick of butter or margarine
- 2 eggs
- ½ cup coconut
- ½ cup and 1 Tbsp mashed pinto beans

- ° 1 tsp vanilla extract
- ° 2 mixing bowls
- ° measuring cups and spoons
- ° potato masher
- ° wooden spoon
- ° electric mixer, hand mixer, or wire whisk
- ° 9-in pie plate
- ° access to an oven
- ° knife

No-Banana Banana Cream Pie
- ° 3 eggs
- ° 2½ cups milk
- ° 6 Tbsp (rounded) flour
- ° ½ cup sugar
- ° 2 Tbsp butter or margarine
- ° ½ tsp salt
- ° 14-oz package of tofu
- ° 1½–2 tsp banana flavoring
- ° 9-in pre-made refrigerator pie crust
- ° 9-in pie plate
- ° round cookie cutter with a 1-in to 1½-in diameter
- ° medium saucepan
- ° measuring cups and spoons
- ° access to an oven
- ° knife
- ° small dish
- ° wooden spoon

Safety and Disposal

Because students will eat the product of this activity, be sure to mix and bake the pies outside the laboratory (e.g., at home, in a home economics laboratory, or in the school cafeteria). Use ingredients, measuring utensils, and baking equipment that is not used in the lab or stored among laboratory chemicals. Impress upon the students that this experiment is an exception to the rule that they should never taste anything used or produced in a chemistry class or other science class.

Getting Ready

If your classroom time is limited, you may wish to bake the pies ahead of time according to the recipes in the Procedure and let the class sample the results. Alternatively, have the students taste pies baked by a previous class.

Opening Strategy

Tell students that all flavors are chemicals, and that the "flavor" of an apple pie involves our tongue's response to the chemicals present in the pie and the texture of pie, as well as our eyes' response to the color of the food, and the nose's response to the spices and other aromas released from the pie. The brain can be fooled if we eat something that resembles an apple pie in flavor and texture.

If you have already prepared the pie, you may wish to conceal the true identity of the pie until after the students have tasted it and commented about its flavor and texture.

Procedure

Use one or more of the following recipes to make sense-fooling pies:

Recipe 1: No-Apple Apple Pie

1. Put the bottom pie crust in the pie plate.

2. Boil 2 cups of water in the large saucepan. When the water boils, slowly add 1½ cups sugar and 1½ tsp cream of tartar. Stir the mixture until the solids dissolve.

3. Add 25 Ritz crackers, one at a time, to the boiling water. Do not break up the crackers. Do not stir the mixture.

4. Boil the cracker mixture for 2 minutes, then remove from heat.

5. Pour the cracker mixture into the crust and sprinkle with 1 tsp cinnamon.

6. Melt a teaspoon of butter or margarine and drip it over the filling.

7. Carefully place the top crust on the pie and press the edges of the crust together. Cut vents in the top crust with a knife.

8. Bake the pie at 425°F (218°C) for 25–30 minutes, or until the crust is golden brown.

9. Let the pie cool for at least 15 minutes or until you can cut it easily. Share it with your students.

Recipe 2: No-Pecan Pecan Pie

1. Drain one can of pinto beans and mash them with a potato masher in a mixing bowl. Measure out ½ cup and 1 Tbsp mashed beans and set aside for use in Step 4. Discard or save the remainder of the beans.

2. In a second bowl, cream together 1½ cups sugar and 1 stick of butter or margarine.

3. Add 2 eggs and mix well.

4. Add the remaining ingredients (½ cup coconut, ½ cup and 1 Tbsp pinto beans, and 1 tsp vanilla extract) and mix well.

5. Put the pie crust in the pie plate.

6. Pour the pie-filling mixture into the unbaked crust.

7. Bake at 350°F (177°C) for 1 hour.

8. Cool before serving.

Recipe 3: No-Banana Banana Cream Pie

1. Bake a pre-made pie crust in a pie plate in a 350°F (177°C) oven for 10 minutes or until the edges of the pie crust begin to turn brown.

2. Open the package of tofu and drain the excess liquid. Place the tofu on a plate and press the cookie cutter through the tofu to get cylindrical sections similar in diameter to a banana. Cut the cylinders of tofu into ⅛-inch-thick slices.

3. Add the following to a medium-sized saucepan:
   - 2½ cups milk
   - 6 rounded Tbsp flour
   - ½ cup sugar
   - 2 Tbsp butter or margarine
   - ½ tsp salt

4. Separate three eggs, saving the yolks in a small dish and discarding the egg whites. Beat the yolks together and set aside for use in Step 6.

5. Heat the ingredients from Step 3 in the saucepan over medium heat, mixing thoroughly. Once the ingredients have been thoroughly mixed, the mixture will begin to thicken.

6. Transfer ½ cup of the thickened mixture from the saucepan into the bowl containing the egg yolks. Stir the thickened mixture and egg yolks together. Return this mixture to the saucepan.

7. Continue cooking the mixture in the saucepan and add 1½–2 tsp banana flavoring to the mixture. Quickly stir the flavoring into the base for 20–30 seconds and remove the saucepan from the heat. This mixture is the pie filling.

8. Use a third of the filling to cover the bottom of the pie crust.

9. Lay half the slices of tofu on top of the filling.

10. Cover the tofu layer with another layer of filling.

11. Add a second layer of tofu slices and top with the remaining filling.

12. Let the pie cool, then refrigerate until ready to serve.

Discussion

- Ask students what advantages there might be to making pies with alternative ingredients.
  Using alternative ingredients may decrease the expense of the pies and allow people with food allergies to enjoy the pies.

- Discuss the flavor and texture of the pie. Ask students whether they think a pie made with the more traditional ingredients (e.g., apples, bananas, etc.) would be better for them, and why or why not.

- Ask students to explain how the senses of smell, sight, and taste help us to taste our food.
  See Explanation for answers.

Explanation

In this activity, pies were made with alternative ingredients that provide the flavor, color, and texture to suggest certain foods. As long as the olfactory sense (smell) detects the appropriate odors associated with that food, the brain can be tricked into thinking that food is what it appears to be although the key ingredients are missing.

The acidic nature of apples give them their characteristic sour taste. In the imitation apple pie, the sour (acid) taste is a result of the reaction between cream of tartar and water to form tartaric acid. Many of the other components that are responsible for the natural flavor of apples are volatile. That is why fruit pies usually taste more bland than the uncooked fruit. The volatile components evaporate from real apple pie when you bake it. Natural apple pie provides more nutritional value than the imitation pie, because apples have vitamins and fiber not found in the crackers. While vitamins can be destroyed by heat, some still remain in the cooked pie.

In a real pecan pie, the texture and consistency of the gel layer are provided by the mixture of the corn syrup, brown sugar, and butter. These ingredients are replaced in the imitation pie by the beans, sugar, and eggs. The chewiness of the upper layer provided by the pecans in the real pie is simulated by the coconut. Also, the bean skins resemble pecan pieces. As with most food, the majority of what we taste comes from the spices and sugar that give the pie its characteristic aroma and taste.

In real banana cream pie, the base of the filling is the same as that used in any cream pie, and the flavor is provided by the addition of bananas to the base. In the imitation pie, the tofu, a bland-tasting substitute for bananas, gives the illusion of banana pieces in the pie base. Since the tofu has little to no flavor of its own, the distinctive banana flavor is provided by adding banana flavoring.

See Activity 1, "Flavors Are Chemicals," and the Content Review for a detailed discussion of the senses of taste and smell.

Key Science Concepts

- senses
- volatile molecules

Cross-Curricular Integration

Language Arts
Have the students write advertisements for the three imitation pies, stressing their advantages over their "real" counterparts.

References

Borgford, C.L.; Summerlin, L.R. *Chemical Activities,* Teacher's ed.; American Chemical Society: 1988.

Freedman, D.H. "In the Realm of the Chemical," *Discover.* June 1993, Vol. 14(6), 68–76.

Hayes, K., Centerville High School, Centerville, OH (contributor of No-Banana Banana Cream Pie recipe).

Lewis, R. "When Smell and Taste Go Awry," *FDA Consumer.* Nov 1991, Vol. 25(9), 29–33.

Esters Are Food Flavorings

What makes a banana taste like a banana? Many natural and artificial flavorings belong to a class of compounds called esters. Esters are produced by a chemical process called esterification, and in this activity, students will have the chance to prepare and examine several synthetic flavorings that are esters.

Recommended Grade Level .... Part 1: 4–8, Part 2: 7–12
Group Size .... 1–4 students
Time for Preparation .... 30 minutes
Time for Procedure: .... Part 1: 25 minutes (+ 1 hour for heating)
                                                            Part 2: 45 minutes

Materials

Opening Strategy

Per Student
- food flavorings

Use several different flavorings. Be sure that each flavoring is given to at least two students.

- cotton ball
- small plastic zipper-type bag or film canister
- tape
- (optional) balloon

Procedure, Part 1

Per Group
- 0.2 g (a large pinch) Dowex® 50x2-100 cation exchange resin
- medium-sized test tube (e.g., 13-mm or 16-mm by 150-mm)
- 2–3 small boiling stones
- sand bath made from the following:
  - fine, clean sand (e.g., fine play sand)
  - 150-mL beaker or similar glass container
- hot plate
- alcohol or metal thermometer that reads at least as high as 150°C
- 50-mL beaker
- 0.8 g potassium carbonate (K_2CO_3)
- 1 or more of the alcohol/carboxylic acid pairs shown in Table 1
- goggles

Procedure, Part 2 (Optional)

Per Group
- 3 or more small test tubes
- 400-mL beaker
- 3 or more 125-mL Erlenmeyer flasks
- Bunsen burner or hot plate

- ring stand and wire gauze (if using a Bunsen burner)
- 1 or more of the alcohol/carboxylic acid pairs shown in Table 1
- test tube holder or pair of tongs
- goggles

Per Class
- 100 mL concentrated sulfuric acid (18 M H_2SO_4) in a glass dropper bottle
- plastic gloves

Variation

- several balloons
- food flavorings
- string

Table 1: Alcohol/Carboxylic Acid Pairs and Resulting Esters

Alcohol	Carboxylic Acid	Ester	Odor of Ester
0.5 mL isoamyl (isopentyl) alcohol	1.5 mL ethanoic (acetic) acid	isoamyl acetate	banana
0.5 mL octanol	1.5 mL ethanoic (acetic) acid	octyl acetate	bitter orange (citrus, orange)
0.5 mL isobutanol	0.5 mL formic acid	isobutyl formate	raspberry
1.0 mL methanol	0.5 mL salicylic acid	methyl salicylate	oil of wintergreen
0.5 mL n-propanol	1.5 mL ethanoic (acetic) acid	propyl acetate	pear

Resources

Most of the chemicals for this activity can be purchased from Flinn Scientific, P.O. Box 219, Batavia, IL 60510-0219, 800/452-1261.

- potassium carbonate—catalog # P0038 for 500 g
- sulfuric acid (18 M)—catalog # S0228 for 100 mL
- methanol—catalog # M0054 for 500 mL
- ethanol—catalog # E0007 for 500 mL
- isobutanol—catalog # I0017 for 500 mL
- isoamyl alcohol—catalog # I0031 for 100 mL
- formic acid—catalog # F0044 for 100 mL
- ethanoic acid (acetic acid)—catalog # A0177 for 100 mL
- salicylic acid—catalog # S0001 for 100 g
- octanol—catalog # Q0018 for 100 mL
- n-propanol—catalog # P0228 for 100 mL

Dowex 50x2-100 cation exchange resin can be purchased from Aldrich Chemical Company, 1001 West Saint Paul Avenue, Milwaukee, WI 53233, 800/558-9160.

- Dowex 50x2-100 resin—catalog # 21,744-1 for 100 g

Safety and Disposal

Goggles should be worn when performing this activity. The concentrated sulfuric acid ($18\,M\ H_2SO_4$) is very corrosive and can cause severe chemical burns if it comes in contact with the skin or eyes. Handle with extreme care. The concentrated sulfuric acid should be dispensed by the instructor. Wear gloves to protect your hands while dispensing the concentrated sulfuric acid. If contact should occur, flush the affected area with water for at least 15 minutes. If contact involves the eyes, seek medical attention immediately while continuing to flush the area with water.

Methanol ("wood alcohol") is very toxic if ingested and can be absorbed through the skin. If contact occurs, rinse the affected area with water. Methanol is also highly flammable and should be kept away from open flames. Methanol should be dispensed by the instructor. Wear gloves to protect your hands while dispensing the alcohol.

The water should be heated and the flame turned off before the test tubes are placed into the water. Alcohols are flammable and should be kept away from the flame or hot plate.

Do not let students smell the esters by holding the flasks under their noses. Instead, have them use the wafting procedure described in Employing Appropriate Safety Procedures.

Only very small amounts of esters are present in foods. In large amounts, esters, including those listed in Table 1, can be toxic. In addition, the crude esters synthesized in this activity may contain significant amounts of toxic impurities. Students should never be allowed to taste products that have been made in the laboratory or in lab glassware.

Getting Ready

Prepare the sand baths by half-filling a 150-mL beaker with sand and warming it to 120°C using a hot plate.

Opening Strategy

Introduce the students to esters by placing a cotton ball with 2–3 drops of each flavoring in a separate small plastic bag or film canister. Number each bag and keep a key of which flavor extract is in each bag. Try to use as many flavoring extracts as possible and make at least two of each scent. Each student should receive a numbered plastic bag. Have the students go around the classroom and try to find other students with the same scent as they have. Once they have found another student with the same scent, have them stay together as a group until each student is in a group. Then explain to students that the different scents are chemicals called esters and are used in food flavorings for cooking and baking.

Another idea would be to put a few drops of vanilla extract into a balloon. Inflate the balloon and tie the end. Pass the balloon around the class to see if the students can identify the odor. Introduce the idea that odors are chemicals. Many chemicals (including vanillin) that have strong odors belong to a class of chemicals called esters. In this activity, students will make esters that may have recognizable odors.

Procedure

Part 1: Using Dowex Beads

1. Place about 0.2 g (a large pinch) Dowex 50x2-100 beads into a test tube.

2. Add the correct number of drops of the desired alcohol and the corresponding carboxylic acid from Table 1 to the beads. (Twenty drops equals approximately 1 mL.)

 Never smell unknown materials by holding them directly under your nose. (Salicylic acid has no odor, and acetic acid is a concentrated form of vinegar with a strong odor.)

3. Carefully smell the contents of the test tube by waving your hand across the mouth of the test tube to push the vapor toward your nose. Describe the odor of the starting reagents and record the observation.

4. Add two or three small boiling stones to the test tube to help prevent the contents of the test tube from frothing during the heating step that follows.

5. Stand the test tube in a sand bath that has been warmed to 120°C. Allow the test tube to heat for about 1 hour.

6. After 1 hour of heating, pour the contents of the test tube into a 50-mL beaker containing 0.8 g potassium carbonate (K_2CO_3).

7. Smell the contents of the beaker (by wafting) and record the characteristic odor of the ester that has been produced. Rinse the contents of the beaker down the drain with water.

Part 2: Using Concentrated Sulfuric Acid (Optional)

 This procedure is NOT recommended for the elementary classroom due to the use of concentrated sulfuric acid (18 M H_2SO_4).

1. Add about 200 mL water to the 400-mL beaker. Heat the water until it boils and then turn off the hot plate or gas.

2. Add 10 drops (0.5 mL) of one of the alcohols from Table 1 to a clean, dry test tube.

3. Add the appropriate amount of the carboxylic acid listed next to the alcohol in Table 1.

 The instructor should dispense the sulfuric acid. If contact occurs, rinse thoroughly with water for 15 minutes. See Safety and Disposal.

4. Add two drops of the concentrated sulfuric acid.

5. Use a test tube holder or pair of tongs to place the test tube in the beaker of near-boiling water. Let stand in the hot-water bath for 5 minutes.

6. Add water to the 125-mL Erlenmeyer flask until it is about ⅓ full. Pour the contents of the test tube from Step 5 into the flask and swirl the flask.

 Never smell unknown materials by holding them directly under your nose. Use the wafting procedure described in Employing Appropriate Safety Procedures. Use EXTREME caution wafting the solution that still contains sulfuric acid.

7. Carefully smell the ester by waving your hand across the mouth of the flask to push the vapor toward your nose. Describe the odor of the sample and record the observation. Rinse the contents of the flask down the drain with water.

8. (optional) Repeat Steps 2–7 for another pair of alcohols and acids from Table 1.

Variation

- Provide some commercial esters (or food flavorings) for the students to smell by placing a few drops of each into a separate balloon. Inflate it and tie the end. Pass the balloons around the class to see if students can identify the odor. Have them compare these flavorings with the compounds formed in the experiment. Some students might recognize the odors, but not be able to identify the exact food flavoring. Make a chart on the blackboard and pool the class results. Reiterate the concept that these odors are chemicals and explain that many chemicals that have strong odors belong to a class of chemicals called esters.

Discussion

- Discuss how the Dowex resin or the sulfuric acid functions in the reactions.
  They both act as catalysts to cause reactions to proceed.

- Ask students why using a natural flavoring (such as chocolate) would sometimes be preferable to using an artificial flavoring.
  Some artificial flavorings can be produced to taste just like the natural flavors, such as oil of wintergreen. Other natural flavorings, such as chocolate, are such a complex mixture of chemicals that scientists have yet to make an artificial flavor that tastes just like the natural one.

Explanation

An ester is formed when a carboxylic acid reacts with an alcohol in a process known as esterification. During esterification the –OH group from the acid combines with a –H from the alcohol, forming H_2O. This reaction typically requires a catalyst to speed it. For decades, concentrated sulfuric acid ($18\,M\,H_2SO_4$) has been used as the catalyst, as in the Procedure, Part 2. Its dehydrating capability makes it effective for this purpose. However, for the same reason, it is very dangerous to use. It can cause severe chemical burns that result from the dehydration of the proteins in your skin. The procedure suggested in Part 1 uses a relatively new and safe acidic material called a cation exchange resin; its trade name is Dowex 50x2-100, and it is manufactured by the Dow Chemical Company. The Dowex resin reacts just as the concentrated sulfuric acid does by scavenging the water produced by the esterification reaction and drives the reaction toward producing the ester. Sample equations for esterification are shown in Figure 1.

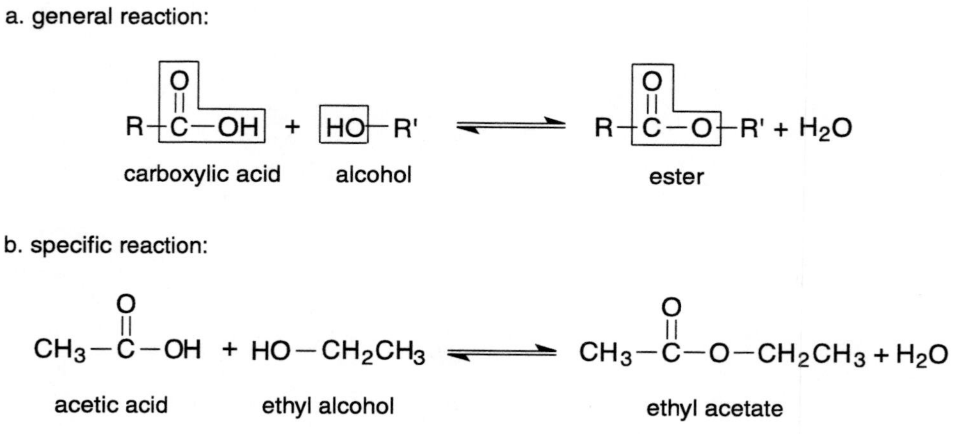

a. general reaction:

$$R-\overset{\overset{\textstyle O}{\|}}{C}-OH \;+\; HO-R' \;\rightleftharpoons\; R-\overset{\overset{\textstyle O}{\|}}{C}-O-R' \;+\; H_2O$$

carboxylic acid   alcohol   ester

b. specific reaction:

$$CH_3-\overset{\overset{\textstyle O}{\|}}{C}-OH \;+\; HO-CH_2CH_3 \;\rightleftharpoons\; CH_3-\overset{\overset{\textstyle O}{\|}}{C}-O-CH_2CH_3 \;+\; H_2O$$

acetic acid   ethyl alcohol   ethyl acetate

Figure 1: The reaction of a carboxylic acid and an alcohol to form an ester

When low-molecular-weight carboxylic acids are esterified, the resulting esters are typically colorless liquids with fruity odors. These synthetic esters are used in the food industry as flavorings. In many cases, the esters produced in the laboratory are the same molecules that give fruits their characteristic flavors. For example, isoamyl acetate, the chemical that gives bananas their characteristic flavor, can be made in the lab by reacting isoamyl alcohol with acetic acid. Other synthetic esters appear to have no natural counterparts. However, they do have fruity flavors that can be used in foods.

Key Science Concepts

- catalysts
- esters

Cross-Curricular Integration

Home, Safety, and Career
Have students use natural and synthetic flavorings in recipes and assess both types of flavorings based on factors such as cost, ease of use, storage life, and quality of taste.

Social Studies
Discuss the impact of artificial flavors and artificial sweeteners on the natural flavorings market. Students could also research other synthetics such as synthetic rubber, nylon, and dyes, and the effect their production has on the markets for their natural counterparts.

Reference

Hershberger, J., Miami University, Oxford, OH, personal communication.

Why Popcorn Pops

5

In this activity, students discover what makes popcorn pop. They also examine the differences in popped volume and moisture content between various brands of popcorn to see if there is any significant relationship.

> **Recommended Grade Level** 4–12
> **Group Size** .... 1–4 students
> **Time for Preparation** .... 1 hour (+ overnight)
> **Time for Procedure** .... 40 minutes

Materials

Procedure, Part 1

Per Class

- hot air or oil popcorn popper
  A hot air popper is preferable. If using an oil popper, additional vegetable oil will be needed.
- access to an oven
- baking sheet
- large mixing bowl
- large measuring cup or 2-L beaker
- 250-mL beaker
- 200 mL (a little less than a cup) unpopped popcorn
- thumbtack, pliers, or food processor
- drinking glass or jar
- paper towel
- clock or watch with a second hand

Procedure, Part 2

Per Group

- 3 brands of popcorn, 20 kernels of each
- 15 mL (1 Tbsp) vegetable oil
- 3 8-cm x 8-cm (3-in x 3-in) squares of aluminum foil
- sharp pencil
- 50-mL graduated cylinder
- 250-mL heat-resistant Erlenmeyer flask (Pyrex® or Kimax®)
- 2 test tube holders
- balance
- hot plate
- 3 containers to hold popcorn brands
- masking tape for labels
- goggles

Safety and Disposal

Goggles should be worn when performing this activity. Students should not be allowed to eat popcorn popped in the laboratory.

Getting Ready

The following steps can be performed at home by the teacher.

1. Preheat oven to 190° F. Spread 50 mL (about ¼ cup) of popcorn kernels in a single layer on a baking sheet. Dry them in the oven overnight.

2. Pour 50 mL (about ¼ cup) of popcorn kernels into a drinking glass or jar. Cover the kernels with water and let them soak overnight. After soaking, dry the kernels on a paper towel and allow them to air dry for about 1 hour. This will allow the pericarp (hull) to dry again, but the kernel itself will have increased water content.

3. Measure 50 mL (about ¼ cup) of popcorn kernels. Break the outer hull of each kernel with a thumbtack or a pair of pliers. You can sometimes break the hulls using a food processor. If using this method, try it out first to make sure that the food processor is really breaking the hulls.

4. Set aside 50 mL (about ¼ cup) of kernels. This will be the "control" popcorn.

5. For Part 2, put the three brands of popcorn into unmarked containers and label them "Brands X, Y, and Z."

Opening Strategy

Ask students if they know why popcorn pops. Ask how popcorn kernels differ from kernels of other kinds of corn that they might have eaten. Explain how the four groups of popcorn were prepared and ask them to make predictions about the results of the experiment (what scientists call a hypothesis).

Procedure

Part 1: The Effect of Moisture Content on Popped Volume of Popcorn

This part of the activity should be performed by the teacher as a demonstration.

1. Explain again to students how the popcorn has been prepared and the procedure that you will use in your demonstration.

2. Pop the "control" popcorn in the popper and catch it in a large mixing bowl. Note the time when the first kernel pops, as well as the time when the majority of the popping has ceased.

3. Use a large beaker or measuring cup to measure the volume of the popped corn. Record this volume along with the popping duration in a data table on the blackboard.

4. Repeat Steps 2 and 3 for the dried, soaked, and punctured kernels. After each type has been popped, let the students make observations about the appearance of the popped corn. If there were unpopped kernels, make note of this too.

If the popcorn preparation was performed with cooking equipment (rather than lab glassware) outside the laboratory, the students may taste the popcorn. Never taste anything that was prepared in lab glassware or in a laboratory room.

5. Using the data table on the blackboard, let the class draw some conclusions about the importance of moisture content in popcorn.

Part 2: Popped Volume and Water Content of Several Brands

 This part of the activity can be done by student groups.

1. Use the 50-mL graduated cylinder to measure the volume of 20 kernels of brand X popcorn. Record this volume.

2. Pour 5 mL (1 tsp) vegetable oil into a clean, dry 250-mL Erlenmeyer flask. Determine the mass of the flask and vegetable oil, and record this mass.

3. Pour the 20 kernels of corn into the Erlenmeyer flask. Determine and record the combined mass of the flask, oil, and popcorn.

4. Make a cover for the flask from aluminum foil. Squeeze the cover tightly around the top of the flask. Use a pencil to poke two or three small holes in the foil.

 Steam escaping from the flask can cause severe burns.

5. Use a test tube holder to hold the neck of the flask. Heat the flask on the hot plate, moving it around so that the kernels do not burn. When the kernels have stopped popping, remove the flask from the heat. Use a test tube holder to carefully remove the foil cover to let the steam escape.

6. After all the steam has escaped and the flask has cooled down to room temperature, weigh the flask and its contents. Record the mass.

7. Pour the popped popcorn into a 50-mL graduated cylinder, measure its volume, and record the volume of the popped corn.

8. Repeat this procedure (Steps 1–7) with brands Y and Z.

9. Calculate the mass of water lost from each brand by subtracting the mass of the popped corn from the mass of the unpopped corn.

10. Calculate the percent water in brand X, Y, or Z using the following formula:

$$\% \ water = \frac{mass \ of \ water \ lost}{mass \ of \ popcorn \ before \ popping} \times 100$$

Discussion

- Discuss why the punctured kernels did not pop.
  If the hull of the kernel is punctured, steam can escape instead of building up the pressure that would cause the kernel to explode.

- Reveal the names of Brands X, Y, and Z popcorn. Discuss which brand yielded the highest volume and the relationship between percentage of water and volume yielded.
  The greater the percentage of water, typically the greater the volume of the popped corn produced. However, water-soaked popcorn has too much water so the volume of popped corn is reduced.

Explanation

Popcorn has been a popular food for centuries. It was first introduced to European settlers by American Indians. The popcorn kernel is the fruit of a corn plant *(Zea mays)*. The hull, or pericarp, of popcorn is hard and moisture resistant. This characteristic of the kernel is important for its popping ability. When the kernels are heated, the water inside boils and turns into a gas (steam). Since gas occupies a much greater volume than a liquid, the pressure inside the hull builds up until it causes the kernel to explode. As the kernel explodes (turning itself inside out in the process), the escaping steam "puffs up" the starchy endosperm material (the food source for the young corn plant), greatly increasing its volume and giving it a spongy, foam-like texture. It might be interesting to compare the texture of popped popcorn to Styrofoam™ "packing peanuts" and discuss how the latter are made. (A gas is forced through the liquid plastic.)

The ability of popcorn to pop depends on the integrity of its hull and the amount of moisture in the kernel. If the hull is punctured, the steam can escape instead of building up the pressure that would cause the kernel to explode. Likewise, if the kernels are allowed to dry out there will not be enough steam to cause an explosion. If the kernel contains too much water, it will not pop as well as kernels that have just the right moisture content. Various brands of popcorn may differ in moisture content due to differences in quality control and packaging. (Poor packaging allows moisture to evaporate from the kernels.)

Key Science Concepts

- pressure
- states of matter

Cross-Curricular Integration

Art
Use the popped popcorn kernels to make mosaic pictures on cardboard or construction paper.

Language Arts
Have the students read the book *The People Shall Continue,* by Simon Ortiz (Children's Book Press, 1988). This book describes the history of Native Americans from a Native American perspective. Corn is mentioned as a staple Native American food.

Mathematics
Have students determine which brand of popcorn is the best value by determining which brand pops the greatest volume for the cost.

Social Studies
The students could use a map of the United States to locate major popcorn-producing states.

Reference

Sibley, L.K. "Popcorn," *ChemMatters.* October 1984, 10–12.

Chemicals Make the Cake

"Chemicals" are not just liquids and powders found in bottles on a laboratory shelf. This activity shows students that chemicals are part of everyday life. They see an example of how the physical characteristics of an everyday item (in this case a cake) are determined by the chemicals from which it is made.

Recommended Grade Level 4–12
Group Size .... 1–4 students
Time for Preparation .... 30 minutes
Time for Procedure .... 90 minutes (including baking)

Materials

Per Group
- ingredients for one of the recipes shown in Table 1

Table 1: Test Cake Recipes

	Ingredients	Recipes				
		A	B	C	D	E
1	table sugar (sucrose)	35 g (2½ Tbsp)	35 g (2½ Tbsp)	45 g (3½ Tbsp)	35 g (2½ Tbsp)	35 g (2½ Tbsp)
2	glucose (dextrose) or fructose	10 g (1 Tbsp)	10 g (1 Tbsp)	—	10 g (1 Tbsp)	10 g (1 Tbsp)
3	vegetable oil (triglyceride)	10 mL (2 tsp)	10 mL (2 tsp)	10 mL (2 tsp)	10 mL (2 tsp)	—
4	shortening (triglyceride)	—	—	—	—	10 g (1 Tbsp)
5	powdered egg white (albumin)	1 g (½ tsp)	1 g (½ tsp)	1 g (½ tsp)	1 g (½ tsp)	1 g (½ tsp)
6	flour (wheat starch)	40 g (⅓ cup)	40 g (⅓ cup)	40 g (⅓ cup)	—	40 g (⅓ cup)
7	corn starch	—	—	—	40 g (⅓ cup)	—
8	Citrucel® (methyl cellulose)	—	—	—	0.25 g (⅛ tsp)	—
9	baking powder	2 g (¾ tsp)	—	2 g (¾ tsp)	2 g (¾ tsp)	2 g (¾ tsp)
10	water	30 mL (2 Tbsp)	30 mL (2 Tbsp)	30 mL (2 Tbsp)	30 mL (2 Tbsp)	30 mL (2 Tbsp)
11	imitation pineapple flavoring (ethyl butyrate)	5 drops	5 drops	5 drops	5 drops	5 drops

- 250-mL Pyrex® or Kimax® beakers (1 for each cake) or aluminum baked potato boats
- pot holders
- 2 paper cups
- measuring cup calibrated in milliliters or graduated cylinder
- a few drops of oil
- spoon or stirring rod
- knife to cut cakes
- (optional) paper cups or plastic bags for distributing ingredients
- (optional) standard 8-inch cake pans

 To make edible cakes in 8-inch pans, multiply all ingredient amounts by five.

Per Class
- balances
- access to an oven
- labels and markers

Resources

Glucose (dextrose) and methyl cellulose can be purchased from a chemical supply company such as Flinn Scientific, P.O. Box 219, Batavia, IL 60510-0219, 800/452-1261.

- dextrose—catalog # D0002 for 500 g
- methyl cellulose—catalog # M00057 for 100 g

It may be difficult to find food-grade glucose if you are making an edible cake. Fructose, which can be found in some grocery stores, can be used instead in the same amount. Powdered egg white can be purchased at a health food store.

Safety and Disposal

Do not let students eat cakes made with laboratory chemicals or in the lab. If you will be eating the cakes, prepare them outside of the lab (e.g., at home, in a cafeteria, or a regular classroom) using food-grade products and cookware.

Getting Ready

Label all of the materials with both the chemical name and the common name. If there are not enough balances available, pre-weigh the solids into paper cups or plastic bags or instruct the class to use volume equivalents provided in the parentheses.

Opening Strategy

Bring in a box of cake mix and read to the class the procedure for preparation and the list of ingredients. Propose to the class the idea that each ingredient is a chemical or mixture of chemicals that are needed to make the cake. Ask the students if all the chemicals (ingredients) are necessary to make the cake. Ask them what would happen if some of the ingredients were omitted. Tell the students that in this activity they will experiment with different cake recipes that omit some of the chemicals. It will be up to them to determine how these chemicals affect the final product.

Procedure

➤ Assign each group one of the recipes listed in Table 1. Recipe A is the control mixture. Each of recipes B–E has one chemical missing or changed. Remind the students that some of the recipes will not use all of the materials provided. Make sure that they check the appropriate column in the table.

1. Label the two paper cups "#1" and "#2."

2. To cup #1, add the appropriate amounts of the first five ingredients (sucrose through egg albumin) as indicated on Table 1.

3. Using a spoon or stirring stick, stir the ingredients in cup #1 for about 1 minute.

4. Add the appropriate amounts of the next four ingredients (wheat starch through baking powder) to cup #2.

5. Using a spoon or stirring rod stir the ingredients in cup #2 for about 1 minute.

6. Pour about half of the contents from cup #2 into cup #1 and stir for 1 minute.

7. Add 30 mL water to cup #1 and stir for 1 minute.

8. Add the remainder of the mixture in cup #2 to cup #1 and stir for 2 minutes.

9. Add 5 drops of imitation pineapple flavoring to the mixture in cup #1 and stir for 1 minute.

10. Put a few drops of oil into the 250-mL beaker and swirl it around so that the bottom and sides are coated.

11. Pour the contents of cup #1 into the beaker. Measure and record the volume of the mixture in milliliters. Label the beaker with the appropriate recipe letter.

➤ **If aluminum baked potato boats are used, calibrate each boat in 50-mL increments by using measured quantities of water and "engraving" marks into the sides of the boat.**

12. Place the beakers in a 350°F (175°C) oven for 25 minutes.

➤ **Place all the beakers in the oven at the same time to keep the temperature from fluctuating excessively.**

13. Use pot holders to remove the beakers from the oven. Measure and record the volumes of the cooked cakes. Compare the heights of the cooked cakes to that of the uncooked heights. Compare the cooked and uncooked heights of different cake mixtures.

14. Remove the cakes from the beakers and cut them in half. Observe the texture, color, and size of the air holes. Compare these observations between cakes made from the different recipes. Record all observations.

Extension

• Compare the five recipes in this activity to the ingredients in prepared cake mixes or to recipes in cook books. Look at recipes for various types of cakes (such as angel food cake, brownies, pancakes, and fruitcakes) and determine how the ingredients contribute to the cakes' appearance and the density of air holes.

Discussion

- Have students determine the differences between the five cake recipes and decide how the change in the recipe changed the appearance of the cake.
  All cakes are compared to recipe A in Table 2.

Table 2: Comparison of Cakes

Cake	Item Missing	Resulting Appearance and Explanation
B	baking powder	Cake is more dense than the others because there was no gas present to make it rise.
C	glucose (dextrose)	Cake was not as brown due to lack of glucose.
D	flour (wheat starch)	Cake rose very high because the corn starch trapped the gas better. It sometimes overflows the beaker.
E	vegetable oil (liquid triglyceride)	Cake rose high and the texture was different. The bubbles in the cake were smaller because the solid shortening shortens the proteins in the flour, trapping smaller gas bubbles.

Explanation

This activity involves preparing cake mixtures with varying amounts of key components. Students follow five different recipes and compare the results. (See Table 2.)

Recipe A is the control mixture. It contains all of the ingredients that a store-bought cake mix would have. After baking it should produce a normal-looking cake.

Recipe B does not include baking powder, a common leavening agent that produces carbon dioxide gas when mixed with water. Other common leavening agents are baking soda (which produces carbon dioxide when mixed with an acidic ingredient in the recipe) and yeast (microorganisms that give off carbon dioxide through the process of respiration when sugar is present in the mixture). A cake made without leavening agents will be flat and dense.

Glucose (dextrose) is one ingredient which may not be familiar to you. It is found in recipe A and in most store-bought cake mixes. Glucose is added to the mix purely for cosmetic reasons. It is a simple sugar that turns brown when exposed to heat. This gives cakes made from store-bought mixes their golden brown color. Since cake C does not have any glucose, it will not be as brown as cakes made from the other recipes.

In recipe D, the flour (wheat starch) is replaced with corn starch and Citrucel (methyl cellulose). These materials will form a much thicker and stickier batter than wheat starch does. Methyl cellulose helps create a structure that can trap the carbon dioxide gas bubbles, making the cake rise more during baking. The matrix that it forms does not allow the cake to flatten when it cools.

Recipe E uses solid shortening rather than liquid oil. This has two effects on the finished cake: it will be slightly taller and will have smaller air pockets than the other cakes. This is because solid shortening can trap gas in its structure, whereas liquid oils cannot. Nitrogen gas is often whipped into shortening in its preparation to make it fluffy. Thus the shortening provides a source of additional gas to the batter. When heated the gas expands, helping the cake to rise more than one made with oil. The size of the air pockets also depends on the shortening's effect on the proteins in flour. These proteins, called gluten (from which we get the word glue), are long chains of molecules that stick together as the batter is heated, forming a network that traps bubbles of gas. (It is the effect of heat on the gluten that causes the cake to become solid as it cooks.) The shortening helps to tenderize the protein in the flour by separating starch granules from the coagulated gluten. Additionally, the shortening helps to make the cake more smooth and moist in the mouth.

Key Science Concepts

- chemical reactions
- scientific method

Cross-Curricular Integration

Home, Safety, and Career
Discuss the need for labeling prepackaged foods. Discuss the benefits and disadvantages of using preservatives and artificial flavors and colors in food.

The Action of Leavening Agents

Have you ever wondered what makes bread and cake doughs rise? Why do some recipes call for baking soda and others for baking powder? Why do you have to keep bread dough in a warm place while it is rising? In this activity, students will examine some of the characteristics of different leavening agents, materials that cause breads and cakes to rise.

Recommended Grade Level **4–12**
Group Size .... **1–4 students**
Time for Preparation .... **15 minutes**
Time for Procedure .... **45–60 minutes**

Materials

Opening Strategy
- samples of baked goods
- cookbooks

Procedure
Per Group
- 1 tsp baking soda (sodium bicarbonate, $NaHCO_3$)
- ¾ tsp cream of tartar (potassium hydrogen tartrate, $KHC_4H_4O_6$)
- ¾ tsp baking powder
- 4 tsp dry yeast
- 4 tsp table sugar (sucrose, $C_{12}H_{22}O_{11}$)
- 2 tsp table salt (sodium chloride, $NaCl$)
- 1 Tbsp cookie crumbs or graham cracker crumbs
- 3 125-mL Erlenmeyer flasks or small glass soda bottles
- at least 6 balloons
- 100-mL graduated cylinder or ¼-cup measure
- measuring spoons (full and fractions of a teaspoon)
- small plastic funnel
- 600-mL beaker or 2-L plastic soft-drink bottle with top cut off
- alcohol or metal cooking thermometer
- warm water (40°C or about 100°F)
- clock or watch with a second hand
- goggles

Safety and Disposal

Goggles should be worn in case the balloon, flasks, or bottles break. Caution students not to eat or drink any of the ingredients or solutions. Solutions may be poured down the drain with large amounts of water.

Opening Strategy

Show students some examples of foods that use leavening agents, such as bread, biscuits, cake, and cookies. Have the students examine each of the samples. Cut them in half to show the texture and the air spaces inside. Look at some cookbooks and determine the types of leavening agents used in various recipes.

Procedure

Part 1: Baking Soda

1. Use a funnel to put ¼ tsp baking soda (sodium bicarbonate, $NaHCO_3$) and ¼ tsp cream of tartar (potassium hydrogen tartrate, $KHC_4H_4O_6$) into a balloon.

2. Put ¼ cup water (about 60 mL) into an Erlenmeyer flask or small glass bottle.

3. Place the end of the balloon over the mouth of the flask or bottle.

4. Lift the balloon to allow the solids to fall into the water.

5. Begin timing when the solids touch the water, and end timing when the balloon is inflated enough to pop up and stand on its own. Record this data.

6. Repeat Steps 1–5 using the same balloon but twice as much baking soda and cream of tartar.

7. Repeat Steps 1–5 using a different balloon and no cream of tartar.

Part 2: Baking Powder

1. Use a funnel to put ¼ tsp baking powder into a balloon.

2. Put ¼ cup water (about 60 mL) into an Erlenmeyer flask or small glass bottle.

3. Place the end of the balloon over the mouth of the flask or bottle.

4. Lift the balloon to allow the solid to fall into the water.

5. Begin timing when the solid touches the water, and end timing when the balloon is inflated enough to pop up and stand on its own. Record this data.

6. Repeat Steps 1–5 using the same balloon but twice as much baking powder.

Part 3: Yeast

1. Use a funnel to put 1 tsp yeast and 2 tsp sugar into a balloon.

2. Put ¼ cup (about 60 mL) warm water (40°C or about 100°F) into an Erlenmeyer flask or small glass bottle. Use the thermometer to make sure the temperature is between 40°C and 50°C.

3. Place the end of the balloon over the mouth of the flask or bottle.

4. Put the flask into the 600-mL beaker or 2-L plastic bottle of warm water.

5. Lift the balloon to allow the solids to fall into the water.

6. Begin timing when the solids touch the water, and end timing when the balloon is inflated enough to pop up and stand on its own. Record this data.

7. Repeat Steps 1–3 and 5–6, using the same balloon. (Omit Step 4.) If the balloon does not inflate within 15 minutes, stop the observations and record the data as "greater than 15 minutes."

8. Repeat Steps 1–6, using a different balloon and replacing the sugar with 2 tsp of table salt (sodium chloride). Record your observations. If the balloon does not inflate within 15 minutes, stop the observations and record the data as "greater than 15 minutes."

9. Repeat Steps 1–6, using a different balloon and replacing the sugar with 1 Tbsp (15 mL) of cookie crumbs. Record your observations. If the balloon does not inflate within 15 minutes, stop the observations and record the data as "greater than 15 minutes."

Discussion

- Ask students to explain why the balloon did not inflate when only the baking soda was added to the water in Part 1.
  The baking soda cannot produce carbon dioxide by itself. It needs cream of tartar (an acidic salt) to produce the carbon dioxide.

- Have students compare the times the balloons took to "pop up" when the original amounts of the baking soda-cream of tartar mixture (in Part 1) and of baking powder (in Part 2) were used, and when twice the amount of these materials were used. Ask them to explain the difference.
  It took less time for twice the amounts to inflate the balloon. This was due to the fact that there was more leavening agent available to produce the gas, so more gas was produced. Since more gas was produced, it took less time to fill the balloon than when the original amount of each agent was used.

- Ask the students to explain why the yeast did not produce any carbon dioxide (in Part 3) when the salt was substituted for the sugar.
  The yeast was not able to metabolize the salt as it did the sugar, so no carbon dioxide was produced.

- Discuss the significance of the elevated temperature in Part 3. Ask for students' ideas.
  The warmer the temperature, the faster the yeast metabolizes the sugar. This is true until the temperature is high enough to destroy the yeast cells by denaturing the proteins in the cells.

Explanation

Leavening agents are substances that produce a gas that makes the dough of baked products rise. Three common leavening agents are baking soda (sodium bicarbonate), baking powder (mixture of baking soda, sodium aluminum sulfate, and calcium dihydrogen phosphate), and yeast. Each produces carbon dioxide, but in a different way.

While sodium bicarbonate dissolves in water, it will not produce carbon dioxide unless an acid is present. In this activity, the acidic material is cream of tartar (an acidic salt). The two solids do not react until dissolved in water. Once dissolved, the baking soda and cream of tartar react to produce carbon dioxide and water as shown in Figure 1.

$$NaHCO_3 \text{ (aq)} + KHC_4H_4O_6 \text{ (aq)} \longrightarrow H_2CO_3 \text{ (aq)} + KNaC_4H_4O_6 \text{ (aq)}$$

sodium   potassium hydrogen   carbonic acid   potassium sodium
bicarbonate   tartrate   tartrate
              (a hydrogen salt)

$$H_2CO_3 \text{ (aq)} \rightleftharpoons CO_2 \text{ (g)} + H_2O \text{ (l)}$$

carbonic acid   carbon   water
                                 dioxide

*Figure 1: Baking soda and cream of tartar react to produce
carbon dioxide and water.*

Baking powder is a mixture of baking soda and two acidic salts: sodium aluminum sulfate
and calcium dihydrogen phosphate. In the solid form, the sodium bicarbonate and acid
salts do not react. However, once dissolved in water, the reaction to release carbon dioxide
gas proceeds. The general equation for this reaction is summarized in Figure 2.

$$HCO_3^- \text{ (aq)} + H^+ \text{ (aq)} \rightleftharpoons H_2CO_3 \text{ (aq)} \rightleftharpoons CO_2 \text{ (g)} + H_2O \text{ (l)}$$

bicarbonate ion   hydrogen ion   carbonic acid   carbon   water
                  from the   dioxide
                  acidic salts

Figure 2: Baking powder dissolved in water produces carbon dioxide and water.

Yeast, a living organism, metabolizes its food (sugar) as humans do. Metabolism is a series
of chemical reactions that occur inside the cells of a living organism with the help of
oxygen gas. In this process, sugar breaks down to form carbon dioxide and water. (See
Figure 3.) The carbon dioxide produced by the yeast causes the dough of baked goods to
rise. (Notice that this reaction is the opposite of photosynthesis where carbon dioxide and
water are converted into sugar.)

$$C_6H_{12}O_6 \text{ (aq)} + 6O_2 \text{ (g)} \xrightarrow{\text{yeast}} 6H_2O \text{ (l)} + 6CO_2 \text{ (g)}$$

glucose   oxygen   water   carbon
                                                              dioxide

Figure 3: Sugar breaks down to form carbon dioxide and water.

Several factors control the amount of carbon dioxide produced by the various reactions.
The first is the kind and amount of leavening agent used. If more leavening agent is added,
there will be more present to react, producing more gas (provided that the other
ingredients needed for the reaction are present in ample amounts).

The second factor affecting the amount of carbon dioxide produced is the time permitted
for the reaction to occur. All other factors being equal, the longer the reaction is allowed to
proceed, the more gas will be produced (until you run out of ingredients).

The third factor affecting the gas production is temperature. In general, the higher the
temperature, the faster the reaction. This happens because molecules move more rapidly at
higher temperatures. The more rapidly they move, the more likely they are to collide with
each other with enough force to cause a reaction. This effect can be seen with the yeast
experiments. In reactions with yeast, however, the temperature must not be raised too high
or the heat will kill the yeast, stopping the reaction.

While not examined in this activity, yeasts can also metabolize their food without oxygen by a process called fermentation. In fermentation reactions, carbon dioxide and ethyl alcohol are produced. This is how yeast is used to make beer, wine, and other fermented products. The chemical equation for alcoholic fermentation is shown in Figure 4.

$$C_6H_{12}O_6 \text{ (aq)} \xrightarrow{\text{yeast}} 6CO_2 \text{ (g)} + 2C_2H_5OH \text{ (aq)}$$

glucose   carbon   ethanol
dioxide

Figure 4: The chemical equation for alcoholic fermentation

Key Science Concepts

- acid/base chemistry
- chemical reactions

Cross-Curricular Integration

Home, Safety, and Career
Discuss the differences between leavening agents and their uses in various recipes. You may even want to substitute baking soda for baking powder in a recipe and observe the results.

Reference

"Cookies and Yeast;" *Fun with Chemistry: A Guidebook of K–12 Activities;* Sarquis, M., Sarquis, J., Eds.; Institute for Chemical Education: Madison, WI, 1991; Vol. 1, pp 33–38.

The Densities of Fats and Oils

Why does oil float on water? The answer involves a property of matter known as density. In this activity, students calculate the densities of several household substances, including fat and vegetable oil.

> **Recommended Grade Level** **4–12**
> **Group Size** .... **1–4 students**
> **Time for Preparation** .... **15 minutes**
> **Time for Procedure** .... **30 minutes**

Materials

Opening Strategy
- 100-mL graduated cylinder, large test tube, or similar narrow container
- 15 mL corn syrup
- 15 mL rubbing alcohol (70% isopropyl alcohol solution)
- 15 mL vegetable oil
- 15 mL water
- (optional) food color

Procedure
Per Group
- balance
- 100-mL graduated cylinder
- 1 of the following:
    - 50 mL water
    - 50 mL rubbing alcohol
    - 50 mL corn syrup
    - 50 mL vegetable oil
    - stick of butter, margarine, or Crisco® shortening
- metric ruler (at least 30 cm)
- (optional) 1-cup (~250-mL) measuring cup

Per Class
- paper towels
- (optional) plastic squeeze bottles (such as shampoo bottles, dishwashing liquid bottles, syrup bottles) for dispensing the liquids listed for the Procedure

Safety and Disposal

Rubbing alcohol (70% isopropyl alcohol solution) is intended for external use only. All solutions (vegetable oil, corn syrup, and rubbing alcohol) can be flushed down the drain with large amounts of water. The solid shortening can be discarded in the waste basket.

Getting Ready

If desired, put the oil, rubbing alcohol, and corn syrup into labeled squeeze bottles from which students can dispense the samples. This will help reduce dripping and spills.

Opening Strategy

To introduce the concept of density to the students, make a density column using common household materials that will also be used in the Procedure. Pour the liquids into a 100-mL graduated cylinder, large test tube, or similar container in the following sequence: corn syrup, water, oil, and rubbing alcohol. You may wish to color the water to make it more visible. Since corn syrup is thick and sticky, try to pour it into the cylinder without allowing it to run down the side. Minimize mixing by pouring the other liquids down the side of the cylinder. Discuss the concept of relative density and use this density column to introduce the activity.

Procedure

This activity is effectively done by dividing the density determinations for the five materials to be tested among five groups. The results of the calculations from each group can be shared with the class.

1. Determine and record the mass of a clean, dry 100-mL graduated cylinder.

2. Carefully pour about 50 mL water into the graduated cylinder. Record the measured volume.

3. Determine and record the mass of the cylinder and its contents.

4. Determine the mass of the water by subtracting the mass of the empty cylinder from the mass of the cylinder and the water. Record the calculated mass of the water.

5. Calculate the density of the water using the formula given below and record the density.

$$density = \frac{mass\ of\ liquid\ or\ solid}{volume\ of\ liquid\ or\ solid}$$

6. Determine the density of rubbing alcohol, corn syrup, and oil by repeating Steps 1–5, being sure to clean and dry the graduated cylinder between samples.

7. Determine the density of a stick of butter, margarine, or Crisco using one of the following methods:

Method 1: Measuring Volume with a Ruler

   a. Determine and record the mass of a stick of butter, margarine, or Crisco.

   b. Measure the length, width, and height of the stick.

   c. Calculate the volume of the stick of butter by multiplying the length times width times height.

   d. Calculate and record the density of the stick of butter.

➤ Method 2: Measuring the Volume by Water Displacement
This method is especially useful for irregularly-shaped solids.

a. Determine and record the mass of a 1-cup (250-mL) measuring cup or beaker half-filled with water. Use the volume calibrations from the measuring cup or beaker to determine the volume of water in milliliters. Record this volume.

b. Add butter, margarine, or Crisco in pieces, chunks, or spoonsful to the water. Record the volume in milliliters from the cup or beaker. Do not add so much solid that it sticks to the sides or projects above the highest mark on the measuring cup or beaker.

c. Determine the volume of the solid by subtracting the volume of water from the volume of the water plus the solid.

d. Determine and record the mass of the measuring cup and its contents.

e. Determine the mass of the solid by subtracting the mass of the cup and water (from Step a) from the mass of the cup, water, and solid (from Step d). Record this mass.

f. Calculate and record the density of the solid.

Discussion

- Have students rank the densities of the four liquids from highest density to lowest density.
  Corn syrup, water, oil, and rubbing alcohol.

- Pose the following challenge: Shortening is typically sold in 500 g amounts. Can a can with a 520-mL volume labeled 500 g be used to package a batch of shortening with a density of 0.95 g/mL and still pass the honesty in labeling test?
  No, this can will hold only 494 g of the shortening.

- Discuss how food companies can use density to monitor their product to ensure that every batch is the same.
  For every batch of product, pick a full can out of the line. The can will have a known volume and mass. Assume the volume of the food is equal to the volume of the can. The mass of the food is determined by subtracting the mass of an empty can from the mass of a full can. Calculate the density of the food and compare it to the desired density for the product. With this comparative density information, the quality control officer can decide if the new batch is within the acceptable range.

Explanation

The density column created in the Opening Strategy was made by layering four different liquids. This was done in a special sequence that placed the most dense liquid in first, the second most dense in second, and so on. The sequence was chosen based on the fact that as long as the substances do not interact, a less-dense substance will float above a more-dense substance. In the density column, corn syrup was on the bottom, then the water layer, the oil layer, and finally the rubbing alcohol (70% isopropyl alcohol solution). Observing a density column of this type allows you to deduce the relative densities of the components. Corn syrup is the most dense of the four, followed by water, oil, and rubbing alcohol in decreasing order of density.

In the density column activity, it is important to note that water, rubbing alcohol, and corn syrup are all soluble in each other. Also, oil is partially soluble in rubbing alcohol. As a result of this, had the rubbing alcohol been added first and then the water, the two liquids would have mixed. Similarly, adding the rubbing alcohol first, followed by the oil, would have allowed some of the oil to dissolve in the rubbing alcohol as it flowed through the rubbing alcohol. (Remember, oil is more dense than rubbing alcohol, and will sink below it.) Thus, one must consider the solubility of one liquid in another as well as the relative densities.

Experimenting with adding the liquids in different sequences can provide some interesting information about the solubility of these liquids as well as the rate at which the dissolving process occurs. Although corn syrup dissolves in water (after all, it is just a concentrated sugar-water solution), the corn syrup can be poured through water, oil, or rubbing alcohol without much observable change. Dissolving is often a slow process, and the syrup is a prime example of this.

The exact densities of the substances used in this experiment can be calculated. Density is a physical property that relates mass to volume. By definition, density is mass divided by volume (mass per unit volume).

$$density = \frac{mass\ of\ liquid\ or\ solid}{volume\ of\ liquid\ or\ solid}$$

The density of a substance is not dependent on the size of the sample. Every pure substance has a density that is always the same at a given temperature. For example, at room temperature, the density of pure water is 1.00 g/mL, the density of corn syrup is 1.37 g/mL, the density of vegetable oil is 0.92 g/mL, and the density of rubbing alcohol is 0.87 g/mL. The density of a pure substance can be used to help identify it and distinguish it from other substances.

Density can be used as an identifying property for food industry quality control. Shortening is produced by mixing together solidified vegetable oil and liquid vegetable oil. In order to make certain that the shortening is made exactly the same each time, chemists measure the density of the mixtures. If the batches are the same, they will have the same density. The process of making sure that all the batches are the same is called quality control.

Key Science Concept

- density
- solubility

Cross-Curricular Integration

Mathematics
Have students collect the data during science class and then calculate the densities of the substances during math class.

Reference

"Household Density Columns;" *Fun with Chemistry, A Guidebook of K–12 Activities;* Sarquis, M., Sarquis, J., Eds.; Institute for Chemical Education: Madison, WI, 1991; Vol. 1, pp 115–118.

The Fat Content of Snack Food

Are snack foods "good" for you? In this activity, students calculate the percent fat present in several types of snack foods.

Recommended Grade Level **10–12**
Group Size .... **1–4 students**
Time for Preparation .... **15 minutes**
Time for Procedure .... **45–60 minutes**

Materials

Procedure

Per Group
- 100-mL beaker
- glass funnel
- 125-mL Erlenmeyer flask
- 50-mL graduated cylinder
- balance
- approximately 5 g of a snack food (potato chips, corn chips, "lite" chips, etc.)
- 50 mL hexane
- filter paper
- paper towels
- plastic sandwich bag
- small ring clamp
- ring stand
- forceps
- glass stirring rod
- (optional) 250-mL beaker
- (optional) 400-mL beaker or dishpan
- (optional) very hot tap water
- goggles

Resources

Hexane can be purchased from a chemical supply company such as Flinn Scientific, P.O. Box 219, Batavia, IL 60510-0219, 800/452-1261.

- hexane—catalog # H0002 for 500 mL

Safety and Disposal

Goggles should be worn when performing this activity. Caution students not to eat anything used in the laboratory.

Hexane vapors can irritate the respiratory tract and can be narcotic in high concentrations. In addition, hexane is extremely flammable. Use hexane only in a fume hood. Any hexane remaining after the activity is completed should be stored for future use. Any used hexane should be collected and left in the hood to evaporate. Any fat or snack food pieces remaining in the beakers/flasks should be discarded in the trash. Any unused snack food should be discarded in the trash.

Opening Strategy

Read the label on the back of a potato chip bag to the class. Discuss how many calories are provided by the snack and how much fat is present in each serving.

Procedure

 Suggest that each group test a different sample, including the "lite" snacks, for comparison.

1. Place about 5 g of a snack food (several chips) in a plastic sandwich bag and close the bag. Crush the chips into small crumbs by smashing them with your hands.

2. Determine and record the mass of an empty 100-mL beaker.

3. Empty the crushed snack food into the 100-mL beaker and determine the mass of the beaker plus the snack food crumbs. Record the mass.

4. Calculate the mass of the snack food by subtracting the mass of the empty beaker from the mass of the beaker and snack food. Record this mass.

 Perform Step 5 and Steps 7–9 in a laboratory fume hood.

5. Measure 30 mL hexane in a graduated cylinder. Add the hexane to the snack food crumbs in the 100-mL beaker and stir for 10 minutes with a glass stirring rod. Use the stirring rod to gently push the crumbs down into the solution to ensure that all surfaces of the crumbs are wet with hexane. Leave the beaker in the fume hood.

6. Determine and record the mass of a piece of filter paper.

7. Set up a filter apparatus in the fume hood using the weighed filter paper, a glass funnel, and a 125-mL Erlenmeyer flask. Attach a small ring clamp to a ring stand and slide the glass funnel through the opening in the ring. Adjust the height of the clamp so that the end of the funnel is inside the Erlenmeyer flask as shown in Figure 1.

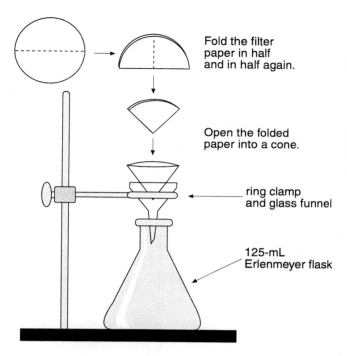

Fold the filter paper in half and in half again.

Open the folded paper into a cone.

ring clamp and glass funnel

125-mL Erlenmeyer flask

Figure 1: The filter apparatus

8. Gently swirl the snack food/hexane mixture in the beaker and pour it onto the filter paper. Add 10 mL hexane to the beaker and swirl again to rinse the beaker. Pour this into the filter paper. Repeat the hexane rinsing a second time in order to get all of the mixture out of the flask.

9. After all the liquid has passed through the filter paper, use forceps to carefully transfer the filter paper and its solid contents onto a layer of paper towels. Allow the paper to dry in the hood until all of the hexane has evaporated. (This should take 20–30 minutes.)

10. Determine and record the mass of the filter paper and its contents. **If the mass continues to decrease as it is measured, the sample is not dry yet. Return the filter paper and solid to a new layer of paper towels in the hood and reweigh after a few more minutes.**

11. Calculate the mass of the snack food after filtration by subtracting the mass of the filter paper from the mass of the filter paper and its contents.

12. Calculate the difference between the original mass of the snack food and the mass of the snack food after filtration. (This difference is the mass of the extracted fat.)

13. Calculate the percent by mass of fat in the snack food, using the following formula.

$$\% \ fat = \frac{mass \ of \ fat}{original \ mass \ of \ snack \ food} \times 100$$

14. Calculate an estimate of the number of dietary calories produced in the digestion of the fat in this snack food sample.

$$dietary \ calories \ from \ digestion \ of \ fat = \frac{9 \ dietary \ calories}{gram \ of \ fat} \times mass \ of \ fat$$

This number can be used to calculate the percentage of calories from fat in this snack food sample.

$$\% \text{ of calories from fat} = \frac{\text{dietary calories from digestion of fat}}{\text{total dietary calories}} \times 100$$

Additional Steps (Optional)

15. Partially fill a 400-mL beaker or dish pan with very hot water from the tap and put it in the fume hood.

 Do not use a hot plate or Bunsen burner to heat the water, as hexane is flammable.

16. Transfer the hexane solution (filtrate from Step 7) from the Erlenmeyer flask into a 250-mL beaker. Place the beaker into the hot water. Make sure that the top of the beaker is above water level, so no water enters the beaker.

17. Allow the hexane solution to sit in the hot water for 10–15 minutes.

18. (optional) Add additional warm water to the 400-mL beaker as the water cools to speed up the evaporation process.

19. After the hexane has evaporated, determine the mass of the fat remaining in the beaker. Record the mass.

Discussion

- Record the results for all the snack food samples on the board. Ask students to rank the different snack foods from highest percent fat to lowest. Ask students if there was a significant difference in fat content between the "lite" snacks and the regular ones.

- Ask students if they will change their eating habits now that they know how much fat is contained in many of the foods that they eat.

Explanation

This activity involves the extraction of fat and oil from snack foods. Fats and oils are the simplest and most abundant kinds of lipids. Lipids are a major category of biochemical molecules that include all biological compounds that are not soluble in water but are soluble in nonpolar organic solvents. While fats and oils are termed the simplest kinds of lipids, they often have large, complex structures which can be intimidating to beginning chemistry students. At the introductory levels it is sufficient to say that fats and oils are nonpolar biochemical molecules that have hydrocarbon sections that are 16 or 18 carbons long. See the Content Review for a more detailed discussion of fats and oils.

The separation done in the activity utilizes the fact that the fats and oils are soluble in hexane. Hexane is a nonpolar organic solvent. Its molecular formula is C_6H_{14}. Because it contains only carbon and hydrogen, it is classified as a hydrocarbon. Chemists use the simple rule, "Like dissolves like" to decide if one substance is soluble in another. This rule means that compounds with similar structures will be soluble in each other. Fats and oils and hexane are nonpolar organic compounds that are hydrocarbons either in total (hexane) or in part (fats and oils).

Fats and oils are used as energy storage molecules for cells. While the body needs fats, oils, and other lipids to function properly, one source of the lipid may be a healthier choice than another. (See the Content Review for a detailed look at the structures of fats and oils.)

Key Science Concepts

- extraction
- fats
- percent composition
- solubility

Cross-Curricular Integration

Home, Safety, and Career
Have students do library research to determine the fat content of some processed and non-processed foods.

Compare the cost of a diet low in saturated fat to the cost of a diet high in saturated fat.

Life Science
Discuss healthy diets. You may want to have the students keep track of the amount of calories and fat consumed over some period of time.

Mathematics
Have students calculate their percent of total calories from fat over some period of time. Compare the results to the recommended 30% or less of total calories from fat.

Social Studies
Discuss diets around the world or diets from the past. Not all people have (or have had) the luxury of choosing diets low in saturated fat.

References

Bloomfield, M.M. *Chemistry and the Living Organism,* 5th ed.; Wiley & Sons: New York, NY, 1992; pp 531–537.

Carle, M.A.; Sarquis, A.M.; Nolan, L.M. *Physical Science: The Challenge of Discovery,* Teacher's ed.; Heath: Lexington, MA, 1991; p T508.

Solubility of Vitamins

If we all need vitamins, why do some bottles of vitamins include the warning "Keep out of the reach of children"? In this activity, students will investigate the two types of vitamins, fat-soluble and water-soluble, and determine how the differences in solubility affect the toxicity of different vitamins.

Recommended Grade Level 4–12
Group Size .... 1–4 students
Time for Preparation .... 30 minutes
Time for Procedure .... 45–55 minutes

Materials

Opening Strategy
- several different packages of vitamins

Procedure
Per Group
- 2 straight pins or safety pins
- 6 small test tubes (13-mm x 100-mm)
- 6 stoppers or corks to fit test tubes
- test tube rack or container to hold test tubes
- ⅛-tsp measuring spoon
- 4 vitamin E capsules
- 4 vitamin A capsules
- ¼ tsp ascorbic acid (vitamin C)
- 15 mL vegetable oil
- masking tape for test tube labels

Resources

Ascorbic acid powder can be purchased from a chemical supply company such as Flinn Scientific, P.O. Box 219, Batavia, IL 60510-0219, 800/452-1261.

- ascorbic acid powder—catalog # A0077 for 25 g

Vitamins E and A and pure vitamin C crystals can be purchased at a grocery store or health food store. In the case of vitamin C, make sure that the ingredients say "ascorbic acid" and not "sodium ascorbate."

Safety and Disposal

All solutions may be flushed down the drain with large amounts of water.

Opening Strategy

Collect several packages of vitamins. Read the labels to the class, including recommended dosage and precautions about overdosage. Ask students why this information might be different for different vitamins.

If possible, invite a health professional to school to discuss use and misuse of vitamins.

Procedure

➤ **Some students may mistake the meniscus of water as a separate layer. (The meniscus is formed when water adheres to the sides of the container forming a concave surface.) Be sure to explain this phenomenon to the students before they begin the Procedure. (See Figure 1.)**

Figure 1: The meniscus formed by water

1. Label a clean test tube "vitamin E + water." Using a pin, poke a hole in two vitamin E capsules and carefully squeeze their contents into the test tube.

2. Label a second test tube "vitamin A + water." Using a second, clean pin, poke a hole into two vitamin A capsules and carefully squeeze their contents into the test tube.

3. Label a third test tube "vitamin C + water." Add a small amount (about ⅛ tsp) ascorbic acid (vitamin C powder) to the test tube.

4. Fill the three test tubes half-full with water.

5. Stopper each test tube. Holding a finger over the stopper, shake each tube vigorously several times. Place the test tubes in the test tube rack or stand them in an another appropriate container, and let them stand for 2–3 minutes.

6. Observe the contents of the test tubes and record any observations. Save the test tubes and their contents as a comparison for Step 8.

7. Repeat Steps 1–6 substituting vegetable oil for water and appropriately labeling the test tubes.

8. Compare the vitamin-water and vitamin-oil mixtures and determine the solubility of each vitamin in both water and vegetable oil.

Discussion

- Ask the students which of the vitamins tested were soluble in water and which ones were soluble in vegetable oil.
  Vitamin C is soluble in water and Vitamins E and A are soluble in oil.

- Discuss how the solubility of the vitamins affects how they are stored in the body.
  Fat-soluble vitamins (such as vitamins E and A) are stored in the body fat, while water-soluble vitamins (such as vitamin C) are not stored.

- Ask students to explain how the manner in which different vitamins are stored influences the desired frequency of vitamin intake.
  Since vitamins like vitamin C are not stored, it is essential that we receive a daily allocation. Vitamins like vitamins E and A can be stored in the fatty tissues, and therefore do not need to be taken every day.

Explanation

Vitamins are small organic molecules essential to maintaining health. Because they are not synthesized by the body in sufficient amounts, vitamins must be a regular part of the diet. Vitamins can be classified as water-soluble (will dissolve in water) or fat-soluble (will not dissolve in water, but will dissolve in oil-like solvents).

The water-soluble vitamins include all the B vitamins (thiamin, niacin, riboflavin, B_6, B_{12}, etc.) and vitamin C. The fat-soluble vitamins include vitamins A, D, E, and K. Water-soluble vitamins are soluble in the blood (which is mostly water). Once in the blood, the water-soluble vitamins end up in the kidneys, where excess amounts of these vitamins are excreted in the urine. This means that water-soluble vitamins are not stored in the body, so they must be present in the daily diet. In contrast, fat-soluble vitamins are stored in body fat. Because any excess of the fat-soluble vitamins is stored, ingestion of large doses of these vitamins can be toxic.

As shown in this activity, vitamins E and A were soluble in the vegetable oil, but not in water. On the other hand, vitamin C was soluble in water, but not in oil. These observations can be explained by examining the structures of the three vitamins as shown in Figure 2.

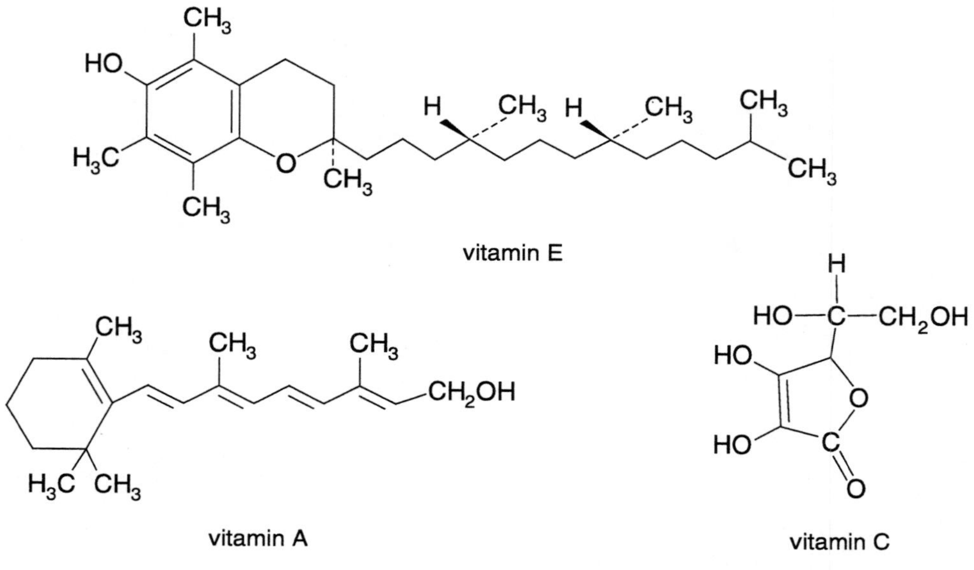

vitamin E

vitamin A

vitamin C

Figure 2: The structures of vitamins E, A, and C

Vitamin C contains many –OH groups. Because of these –OH groups, water is attracted to the molecule and can therefore dissolve it. The structures of vitamins E and A consist primarily of carbons and hydrogens. They do not contain the high proportion of –OH groups that vitamin C has, and therefore, vitamins E and A are not soluble in water. In chemistry, the saying "like dissolves like" is used to explain the fact that molecules that are chemically like water (H–O–H) dissolve in water, and molecules that are chemically like vegetable oil (mostly carbons and hydrogens) dissolve in vegetable oil.

Key Science Concepts

- solubility
- vitamins

Cross-Curricular Integration

Life Science
Discuss the role of vitamins in the diet. Also discuss problems resulting from vitamin deficiency and vitamin overdose.

References

Bloomfield, M.M. *Chemistry and the Living Organism;* Wiley and Sons: New York, NY, 1987; pp 535–541.

Kroschwitz, J.I.; Winokur, M. *Chemistry—General, Organic, Biological;* McGraw-Hill: New York, NY, 1985; pp 742–744.